The Genial Idiots

The Genial Idiots

The American Saga As Seen by Our Humorists

RICHARD CURTIS

CROWELL-COLLIER PRESS, NEW YORK
COLLIER-MACMILLAN LIMITED, LONDON

 Library of Congress Catalog Card Number: 68-22815. The Macmillan Company, New York. Collier-Macmillan Canada Ltd., Toronto, Ontario. Printed in the United States of America. First Printing.

ACKNOWLEDGEMENTS

Excerpt from *Treadmill to Oblivion*, copyright 1954 by Fred Allen, reprinted with the permission of Atlantic-Little, Brown & Company.
Excerpt from *The Good New Days*, copyright © 1962 by Merriman Smith, reprinted by permission of the publishers, The Bobbs-Merrill Company, Inc.
Excerpt from *Election Day Is a Holiday* by Ogden Nash. Reprinted by permission of Curtis Brown, Ltd. Copyright © 1932, 1960 by Ogden Nash. Originally published in *The New Yorker*.
Excerpt from "Go Josephine, In Your Flying Machine" copyright © 1960 by McCall Corporation. From *The Snake Has All the Lines* by Jean Kerr. Reprinted by permission of Doubleday & Company, Inc.
Excerpts from "How to Understand International Finance" and "The Real Public Enemies" by Robert Benchley from *The Benchley Roundup*, selected by Nathaniel Benchley. Excerpt from "Call for Mr. Kenworthy" from *Inside Benchley* by Robert Benchley. Reprinted by permission of Harper & Row, Publishers, Inc.
Excerpt from *Revelations of Dr. Modesto* by Alan Harrington. Reprinted by permission of Alfred A. Knopf, Inc.
Excerpt from *The Most of A. J. Liebling* by A. J. Liebling. Reprinted by permission of Alfred A. Knopf, Inc.
"One" from *No But I Saw the Movie* originally appeared in *The New Yorker*. Copyright 1951 by Peter DeVries, and reprinted with the permission of Little, Brown.
Excerpt from *Let the Crabgrass Grow* by H. Allen Smith. Copyright © 1948, 1960 by H. Allen Smith, and reprinted by permission of Harold Matson Co., Inc.
Excerpt from *How To Succeed With Women Without Even Trying* by Shepherd Mead. Reprinted with permission of Scott Meredith Literary Agency, Inc.
Excerpts from *Catch-22* by Joseph Heller, copyright © 1961. Reprinted by permission of Simon & Schuster, Inc.
Excerpt from *Acres and Pains* by S. J. Perelman, copyright © 1958. Reprinted by permission of Simon & Schuster, Inc.
Excerpt from *In One Head and Out the Other*, copyright 1951 by Roger Price. Reprinted by permission of Simon & Schuster, Inc.
Excerpt from "The Secret Life of Walter Mitty" in *My World and Welcome to It*. Copyright 1942 by James Thurber. Published by Harcourt, Brace & World, N.Y. Reprinted by permission of Helen Thurber.
Excerpt from *I Chose Capitol Punishment* by Art Buchwald. Reprinted by permission of The World Publishing Company.

This book is dedicated to my family—including the memories of my Father's Father and my Mother's Mother—from whom I learned about laughter

PICTURE CREDITS

The Bettmann Archive, Inc., 81, 116; Culver Pictures, Inc., 3, 14, 50, 65, 74, 106, 140; Historical Pictures Service—Chicago, 34, 37, 84, 99, 112; United Press International, 27, 132–133, 165, 173; University of North Carolina, 26.

Foreword

THIS BOOK IS NOT A HUMOROUS HISTORY OF THE UNITED States. Rather, it is a history of the United States as seen by its humorists. It will not tell you what *I* found funny, but what our men of wit found funny.

As it is not a lengthy work, it touches only on what I believe to be the highlights of American development. I have concentrated on our literature, rather than on the performing media such as radio, movies, television, or the stage; but wherever those media reflect our national humor I have included them. For the most part, though, the examples used in this book are what critics like to call "mainstream" literature.

The American humor, like the rest of the American experience, has a rhythm that ebbs and flows with the expansions, consolidations, and contractions of our growth. And while the rhythm can't be oversimplified, a few general remarks can be made about it. Americans are a restless people. They like things as they are, but not for too long. Around the time they are becoming satisfied, they begin dreaming and longing for what they don't have. When they get that, and have had it for a while, they begin to tire of it and grow anxious to move on.

That is the American rhythm, and while it is what makes our country great, it is also what makes it funny. You would think that after some three and a half centuries of history, to say nothing of the lessons that Old World history can teach us, we would be convinced that progress does not guarantee improvement; it only guarantees change. But we do not seem to be convinced, and we go on striving for progress, hoping that tomorrow will bring not only a change for the better, but perfection itself—paradise on earth.

American society has changed turbulently in three hundred and fifty years, but while the voices that have spoken for it have varied vastly from one age to the next, they seem to have one theme in common. And that is that whatever changes may come and go, the human animal has been, is, and will be pretty much the same as he was when he first started recording his sentiments millennia ago. The man with the soul of a humorist knows that to be true, and when he looks upon the struggles of his fellow men to convert their world into paradise, what else can he do but laugh? *That* is the Big Joke, the one that all the humorists represented in this book are laughing about. Perhaps paradise on earth will come only when the rest of us find it funny too. To help Americans realize that dream this book will be devoted.

R. C.

New York, N.Y.
New Year's Day 1968

Contents

Part I
The Laughter of Innocence

Part II
The Laughter of Maturity

Part I:

The Laughter of Innocence

1

The Mirth of the Puritans

PERHAPS THE REASON WHY SO MANY GHOST TALES COME out of New England is that our Puritan forebears are turning in their graves over the injustice done their sense of humor. For of all the misconceptions we hold about our heritage, the most difficult to abandon is that the pilgrims hardly ever laughed. The reason for this misconception has puzzled many scholars familiar with our early culture. But in spite of the massive evidence they have compiled to the contrary, too many of us like to think of our forefathers—and foremothers—as dreary folk garbed in grays and duns, laboring without relief from before cockcrow till long after sunset, dining on bland food, taking no entertainment or alcoholic spirits, living only for the Sabbath, and squeezing prayers into every cranny of their existence.

While there is much validity in this description, we have let ourselves be too firmly guided by a special meaning of the word "Puritan," which applied only to a minority of Protestants of the sixteenth and seventeenth centuries who practiced fanatical austerity. Hundreds of years later the term became popular as an easy description of the prudery known as mid-Victorian morality. Thus, "Puritan" has stuck as defining an inhibited person who despises any spontaneous display of joy.

It is a dreadful distortion composed of a number of poorly digested scenes from American history. The French call it a *pastiche,* a work of art consisting of pasted-on fragments of other art works plus some worthless scraps. Inspect this much-cherished pastiche of the Puritan. Here you will see the broad-brimmed hat and buckled shoes of the Dutch patroons; there you will see one of those grotesque primitive paintings of an American child with the face of a decrepit elder; here you will see the eighteenth-century minister Jonathan Edwards preaching a sermon on the fiery doom awaiting evildoers in his congregation; there you will see Roger Williams huddled in a freezing cell awaiting deportation for his heresies; there you will see Hester Prynne, heroine of Hawthorne's *The Scarlet Letter,* scorned by the citizens of Salem for her unspeakable sin; here a touch of a Washington Irving ghost story, there a snatch from one of Poe's horror tales, and the picture is complete—but completely false.

It is said that two half-truths make one whole lie. Our understanding of early colonial life is composed of many half-truths, and whatever our reasons for believing them, we owe it to the restless spirits of our ancestors to set the record straight. For humor was *not* alien to the original Puritans, the religious sect that arose in the early 1500's in reaction to corruptions, abuses, and apostasies that had set into the administration of the Anglican Church and the conduct of its services. It is true that the Puritans wanted to purge the Church of these impurities, but few of them held that laughter—except wicked laughter at God's ways—was an evil influence. They celebrated the festive holidays such as Christmas with as much cheer as other Christians, and although they had

Puritan revellers at Christmas.

much to be grim about because of the persecutions they endured in England and the hardships they suffered in America, their response to such woes was not always sour. It is in fact the very good humor they pitted against adversity that established a style for generations of Americans to emulate.

Some years before John Winthrop led what has been called the "Great Migration" of Puritans in 1629, a Puritan minister in England named Richard Bernard delivered a sermon to his congregation entitled "The Isle of Man." "There is a kind of smiling and joyful laughter, for anything I know," Bernard said, "which may stand with sober gravity, and with the best man's piety." He pointed out that there was not only nothing wrong with being "Christianly merry," but it was even necessary to anyone who wanted to lead a well-rounded religious life. So popular was Bernard's sermon that it went through eleven editions, and it would not be surprising if copies of it were packed among the possessions of the twenty-five thousand or so English immigrants who disembarked on America's shores in the 1630's.

Certainly, too, when Puritan opposition in England gained momentum in the 1640's and started hurtling towards the beheading of Charles I and the emergence of Oliver Cromwell as England's Lord Protector, New England's settlers must have waited hungrily for ships bearing news from the mother country. When those ships arrived they bore the prose satires of John Milton, the poetic genius who had taken it upon himself to speak for the convictions of Cromwell and his ruling Puritan regime. "Jesting," Milton had said, translating the Roman poet Horace, "decides great things Stronglier, and better oft than earnest can." Milton declared that his jesting sought "to rip up the wounds of Idolatry and Superstition with a laughing countenance."

His "The Readie and Easie Way to Establish a Free Commonwealth" ridiculed the principle of divine rights of kings, especially if kings, abusing their privileges, became tyrants:

> What madness is it for them who might manage nobly their own Affairs themselves, sluggishly and weakly to devolve all on a single Person; and more like Boys under Age than men, to commit all to his patronage and disposal, who neither can perform what he undertakes, and yet for undertaking it, though royally paid, will not be their Servant, but their Lord? How unmanly must it needs be, to count such a one the breath of our Nostrils, to hang all our felicity on him, all our safety, our well-being, for which if we were aught else but Sluggards or Babies, we need depend on none but God and our own Counsels, our own active Vertue and Industry.

These satires, so readily absorbed into the cultural life of the American Puritans, not only served to entertain and sustain them, but helped form the foundation of every educated colonist's library. Upon that foundation Benjamin Franklin and his colleagues would build their own satires in the next century, and direct Milton's arguments against another king abusing his privileges.

Milton's works were rather ponderous, of course, but lest we think that such weighty humor is all that the pilgrims had to make them laugh, it should be pointed out that another type of literature they held dear and read avidly were—joke books! In those days they were called "jest books," and were somewhat similar to humor anthologies published today. They contained poems, excerpts from essays and stage works, witty epigrams, and proverbs. *Witts Recreations*, *The Book of Jests*, and *Witts Cabinett* are frequently referred to in inventories of mid-seventeenth-century book owners. And astonishingly, many of the jokes we believe were made up yesterday —jokes of the "Why did the chicken cross the road?" and "Who was that lady I saw you with last night?" variety—were found in those collections. Some of them in fact were surprisingly bawdy. Moderns who persist in associating the word "Puritan" with shame about bodily functions and sex would have their eyes opened by thumbing through these books; some of the material in them is scarcely repeatable on a Sunday evening television variety show.

Jest books became a commonplace in the first hundred years of our colonial life, bringing endless cheer to lonely, desolated souls for whom the Bible and psalm books were not completely satisfying. Comedians of today have expressed amazement at the rapidity with which a new quip crosses the country, but in the colonies, too, a new joke passed from mouth to mouth like a courier on horseback, bringing people who were otherwise strangers into bonds of instant amity. Men with good memories and storytelling talent carried jokes in their heads as they carried merchandise in their bags. Such itinerant comics, resembling the strolling bards of yore, established the pattern out of which were to emerge the traditions of the humorous lecturers of the nineteenth century and the so-called "stand-up" comedians of the twentieth: whom Mark Twain styled collectively The Genial Idiots.

It can be said that jest books and almanacs—the first of the latter was printed in America as early as 1639

—constituted the springs from which the mighty river of American wit was to flow. When we understand the popularity of these books, it becomes easy to understand why, a century later, Joe Miller's *Jests*—a collection published after the death of the well-known English actor—caused a sensation in the colonies and went through countless reprints in an Americanized edition called *The Joe Miller Joke Book*. And also why Ben Franklin's *Poor Richard's Almanac* met with such an enthusiastic response around the same time.

Jest books and almanacs aside, the most important literature read by the Puritans was religious: the Bible, the hymn book, the prayer book, the psalm book, collections of sermons, and popularized stories from the Scriptures. But, as we have seen, few pilgrims held that the service of worship need be relentlessly unsmiling, or that acts of prayer and expressions of faith need be without their light side. The title page of the *Bay Psalm Book*, their most important text outside the Bible, featured this line from James 5:13: "If any be afflicted, let him pray, and if any be merry let him sing psalmes." Ministers did not avoid, as the bases for their sermons, some of the gayer passages in the Good Book. The Reverend Benjamin Colman of Boston often preached that the road to salvation need not be an uphill path through murky theological thickets guarded by avenging beasts. It could also be a jolly romp down a flowery hill. He cited such texts as Psalm 126: "Then was our mouth fill'd with Laughter, and our Tongue with Singing."

Colman actually went so far as to have published a collection of sermons called *The Government and Improvement of Mirth*, in which he said:

> We daily need some respite & diversion, without which we dull our Powers; a little intermission sharpens 'em again. It spoils the *Bow* to keep it always bent, and the *Viol* if always strain'd up. Mirth is some loose or relaxation to the labouring Mind or Body. . . . 'Tis design'd by nature to chear and revive us thro' all the toils and troubles of life.

Colman drew a distinction between good mirth and bad. The bad was overindulgence in any form of pleasure, while the good was a balanced good nature governed by the Golden Rule. The very highest form of mirth was a kind of religious ecstasy, such as that experienced by certain saints and martyrs:

> Especially *Spiritual Joy* is the peculiar Duty and Privilege of Saints: They are under Bonds to exhibit the Pleasures and *Satisfactions of Religion,* if it is possible to convince the Ungodly how *Superior they are* to all those of *Sense* which this World has to boast of. If men are for *Mirth, This* is worthy to be called so and aspir'd after! A Joy that is Solid, Pure, Perfective, Permanent! Stronger than all Afflictions, and abiding in Death! A light in those shades, and a Triumph o'er those Terrors!

Going from the sublime to the less-than-sublime, many ministers employed humor in their services simply as a way of holding attention. Though we think of the pilgrims as devout without exception, a preacher then had the same problem a preacher has today: how to keep his congregation from drifting off into slumberland. Not a few, then, used jokes and gimmicks for this purpose. A story is told of a journeying minister who was asked to deliver a sermon at his friend's church. The friend was desperate because the congregation had a habit of leaving before the service was ended. The visiting minister pursed his lips, then smiled as if infused with a divine inspiration. That Sunday he rose before the congregation, introduced himself, and announced: "I will be addressing two kinds of people at this meeting: sinners and saints. The first half of my sermon will be directed at the sinners, who are free to leave when that portion is finished. Then I will conclude with a talk to the saints." At the conclusion of the first half of his sermon—a vitriolic attack on wickedness—he smiled benignly and gave sinners in the audience their opportunity to leave. None did, however. The entire congregation of saints stayed on for *their* half of the sermon.

When Puritan ministers sought mirth, however, it wasn't always of the religious variety. They enjoyed their fun in a number of ways, and not a few found it in rather substantial quantities of wine. One minister, John Wise, was a huge man and liked to wrestle. A friend of his rode out to Wise's house one day and challenged him to a match. In a few moments it was all over, with the challenger sprawled on the road in front of the cottage: Wise had tossed him clear over his wall. "If you'll just throw my horse after me," the poor fellow cried, dusting off his trousers, "I'll be on my way back to town."

Other ministers diverted themselves by composing anagrams, satirical poems, witty epitaphs, and essays, some of which—though merely in the fashion of the day—might bring horrified blushes to the cheeks of modern seminarians. A few ministers attempted humor of a weightier and less indecent nature, the best of which ranked with some of the best then being produced across the sea.

Foremost was Nathaniel Ward, who served the congregation at Agawam—now Ipswich—in Massachusetts between 1634 and 1638. Much of Ward's work was of a serious nature; he might even be called one of our earliest founding fathers, having been instrumental in codifying New England's civil law. But he is best known for his book *The Simple Cobler of Aggawam* [sic] *in America*, not only because it was delightful on its own merits, but also because it was the first important work in a uniquely American genre. The "simple cobler" initiated the tradition of simple, but honest and shrewd country folk who, assuming an air of wide-eyed innocence, strike at the heart of stupidity, corruption, vanity, and vice with their humble opinions. Ward, calling himself an "uplandish Rusticke," issued his homely convictions on a variety of subjects large and small, and even had something to say about women's fashions:

> To speak moderately, I truely confesse, it is beyond the ken of my understanding to conceive, how those women should have any true grace, or valuable vertue, that have so little wit, as to disfigure themselves with such exotick garbes, as not only dismantles their native lovely lustre, but transclouts them into gant bar-geese, ill-shapen shotten shellfish, Egyptian Hieroglyphicks, or at the best into French flurts of the pastery, which a proper English woman should scorn with her heeles: It is no marvell they wear drailes on the hinder part of their heads, having nothing as it seems in the fore-part, but a few Squirrills braines, to help them frisk from one ill-favor'd fashion to another.

Out of what we now call cracker-barrel wisdom was to emerge an essential characteristic of our native humor. We would see it again and again in the history to come: in the coonskin cap Ben Franklin sported in the salons of Paris; in the squirrel-guns American patriots pitted against the well-wrought arms of English troops; in the cornfed diplomacy of Abe Lincoln; the affected innocence abroad of Mark Twain; the horseback political essays of Will Rogers; and in many, many other ways. For what was beginning to show itself, even in the earliest days of our national history, was a conviction that the roughest-hewn of American bumpkins possessed more wisdom and virtue than a legion of polished Europeans or Americans trying to imitate polished Europeans. The colonies were beginning to simmer with the notion that the presence of a new land would demand more than the mere transfer of customs and traditions from the old one. They were beginning to percolate with the realization that a new chance was offering itself to the world, a chance to remake itself in the pristine forests of the American continent, a chance to cast off not simply the customary women's fashions, but fashions in thought, in taste, in deed. In short, an American vision was being forged in the feeble little colonies that clung to the Atlantic shore. And foresighted men with a sense of humor, like Nathaniel Ward, were beginning to see, with that vision, just how inappropriate all the old fashions were in their new home.

2

The Hoax Artist

ON THE MORNING OF APRIL FOOL'S DAY, 1722, JAMES Franklin of Boston, printer and publisher of *The New England Courant*, opened the door of his shop and kneeled to pick up the variety of communications he invariably found at his feet. These had been slipped under his door the previous night and consisted of news scraps, announcements, advertisements, and no doubt a few more invoices than he cared to see. For the most part, however, they were letters addressed to him for publication in his paper.

Many of these letters merely tattled on prominent figures about town: the postmaster, a minister, a member of the city government; others satirized traditional foibles: pomposity, greed, irreverence, and the like; and a few others took a serious position on issues of the day:

trade, politics, finance, religion. Not many contributors used their own names. Instead they submitted their writings under such colorful pseudonyms as Fanny Mournful, Tom Penshallow, Ichabod Henroost, and Abigail Afterwit.

But one of the submissions was signed by a name unfamiliar to James Franklin: Mrs. Silence Dogood. Explaining that she was the widow of a minister, she declared her intention to entertain readers of the *Courant* once every fortnight with her reflections on a variety of topics.

Examining the handwriting, James had a feeling he had seen it before; and he was fairly certain that Silence Dogood was no more a lady than the King of England was. But it didn't matter. If Mrs. Dogood's contributions were stimulating, her real identity wasn't important. Later that morning he handed the letter to his apprentice Benjamin and ordered him to set it into type for the April 2 edition. Benjamin, a rascal who was always smiling to himself over some piece of mischief or another, seemed especially pleased with himself as he accepted the Dogood paper. James frowned, probably reflecting that if Ben weren't his younger brother, and a pretty good printer's apprentice, he'd be just as happy to send the rogue packing. The word "devil" used to describe such apprentices had probably been coined with a scamp like Ben in mind.

Thus on April 2, 1722, Benjamin Franklin's first printed work appeared, under the not entirely whimsical name of Silence Dogood. It was not only a good hoax on Benjamin's big brother, but a good feature of the newspaper. Other Dogood papers followed every two weeks,

Benjamin was always smiling to himself over some mischief.

launching the public life of the man who, among all his other accomplishments, would also become the foremost American wit of the eighteenth century. At the same time it launched the public life of American letters, because Franklin was the first American writer to be read seriously beyond our shores.

Like many other essays published in the *Courant* and sister papers throughout the colonies, Franklin's Dogood papers were written in a style obviously derivative of Joseph Addison's *Spectator,* which arrived regularly from England along with cloth, manufactured goods, and other products of that refined culture across the sea. Still heavily dependent on the mother country for cultural as well as material imports, these seaboard settlements produced little in the way of literary humor that didn't resemble the urbane wit of the super-civilized London newspapers, of which the *Spectator* was the most fashionable. And Franklin, in his *Autobiography,* would unashamedly confess his debt to Addison, having imitated him and consciously practiced his style until Franklin fancied that, here and there, he had improved on Addison's.

To begin with, Mrs. Dogood chose to pick on the aristocratic school system of Boston, particularly Harvard College, whose gates Franklin saw as guarded by Riches and whose temple was presided over by Learning. The sixteen-year-old apprentice, taking keen pride in having educated himself, exhibited just a little smugness in describing the foot of the temple stairs as thronged with young "beetle-skulls" mingling with Idleness and Ignorance. Occasionally these young fools attempted to rise a bit higher by clinging to the coattails of true scholars; but even if they succeeded they rarely, after graduation, applied to life the lessons they'd learned.

> I reflected in my mind [Mrs. Dogood concludes] on the extreme folly of those parents who, blind to their children's dullness and insensible of the solidity of their skulls, because they think their purses can afford it will needs send them to the Temple of Learning, where, for want of a suitable genius, they learn little more than how to carry them-

> selves handsomely and enter a room genteelly (which might as well be acquired at a dancing-school), and from whence they return, after abundance of trouble and charge, as great blockheads as ever, only more proud and self-conceited.

Franklin was reiterating a theme that, as we have seen from Nathaniel Ward's *Simple Cobler of Aggawam* [sic], was already the most important characteristic of the American temperament. It was a sturdy individualism that boasted that any honest, natural, self-made man could run circles around the foppish pedant or the effete gentleman. Today we call this idea anti-intellectualism, but that is an inaccurate term. Certainly Benjamin Franklin, who could hold his own with the so-called Encyclopedists of France and the towering intelligentsia of England, did not despise learning and study. But what he did despise, with the scorn of a deerskin-garbed backwoodsman, was the pretense to erudition that deluded men into believing themselves too good for common people, common occupations, and common pleasures. It was really anti-snobbery that Franklin was proclaiming; and the lusty American contempt for pomposity that blossomed like a wildflower along our western frontier was as much a Franklin trait as the thrift and common sense for which he is better known.

Young Ben Franklin, writing his righteous little essays under the Silence Dogood pseudonym, was in his way a symbol of the colonial character. We had youth, we had ambition, we had vigor, and we had good ideas; but we had no experience in the New World. As a result we were heavily dependent on our traditions to guide us in our behavior. We wanted to speak in our own voice, a voice suited to the American experience, but because we were still uncomfortable here, because so many of us were transplants from European soil rather than home-grown originals, we could express ourselves only in the old voice. Thus Ben Franklin expressed his hopes that the new land would not become the home of old vices—but he expressed these hopes under someone else's name, imitating someone else's style.

While Franklin would eventually abandon the pseudonym and declare himself in his own name, he was never completely to cast off the powerful English heritage that molded his views or the Addisonian mode in which he expressed them. It is only by realizing that he never cancelled his debt to his European background that we can fully appreciate Franklin. His dividedness was the very source of his wisdom and humor, as it was the source of America's. Until we *did* find our own voice, we would have to modulate between the old and the new. Benjamin Franklin was the foremost master of this technique in the eighteenth century.

By 1723 his differences with his brother led them to the breaking point. He removed to Philadelphia where, after a voyage to London to augment his growing skill as a printer, he thrust himself into the commercial, intellectual, and political life of the rapidly growing city. By 1732 he was already a highly esteemed member of the community, having founded a chain of newspapers in Pennsylvania, Rhode Island, and South Carolina. He was official printer for the Pennsylvania government, had his hand in other printing and stationery enterprises, and had even published some books.

But it was at the end of this year that he was to start

a publishing venture that would achieve as much as any single vehicle for recording, disseminating, and unifying the American voice from border to border, and infusing it with a vitality uniquely its own.

Of course, when he initiated *Poor Richard's Almanac*, as he called it, he had no such noble purpose in mind. Almanacs, it will be recalled, were proven money-makers for printers of that day, and Franklin's hope was simply to capture part of the market. But his genius prevented him from issuing a mere copycat version of these volumes of prediction, advice, folk wisdom, and factual information. He ransacked his library for witty, pointed sayings and converted them to suit the American tongue and temperament. He did not hesitate to modify Bacon, Swift, Rabelais, or even Pope to achieve his purpose.

Whether original, borrowed, or rewritten, the maxims in *Poor Richard* were collected later into one volume entitled *The Way to Wealth*, which constitutes one of the greatest collections of its kind ever published. Among the maxims that guided his contemporaries—and might guide ours as well—were:

An empty bag cannot stand upright.

Experience keeps a dear school, yet fools will learn in no other.

Three may keep a secret if two of them are dead.

Creditors have better memories than debtors.

Considerably more than mere clever turns of phrase, they were aimed at instructing and uplifting by entertaining:

Keep your eyes wide open before marriage, half shut afterwards.

None preaches better than the ant, and she says nothing.

Write with the learned, pronounce with the vulgar.

Let thy maidservant be faithful, strong, and homely.

The twenty years or so following publication of the first *Poor Richard's Almanac* were to witness the ascent of Franklin's star to the very crown of the colonial firmament. Entering the public affairs of his colony and city on a larger scale than ever before, he became in 1736 clerk of the Pennsylvania legislative assembly, and in the following year, while retaining that post, was appointed postmaster of Philadelphia, a key position placing him at the crossroads of the colonial communications network. He also strove to advance the cultural life of his community, forming the Junto, or Leather Apron Club, a society devoted to discussing political, religious, philosophic, and economic questions, and to disseminating information domestically and abroad. Using the influence gained from his public and private associations, he was able to lead an enormous number of important projects, such as organizing a volunteer fire company, founding an academy of higher learning which would become the University of Pennsylvania, establishing a volunteer militia, instituting a subscription library, and constructing a hospital and medical school. With all this, he was still able to pursue his scientific inclinations, which resulted in his famous accomplishments in physics and other sciences.

But it was the period after 1751 that concerns us most. During that time his allegiance expanded from Philadelphia to Pennsylvania to America, paralleling the course of his country as the loose association of towns and colonies began to bind together, first as a confederation, then as a nation. And as America bloomed into independence, as a republic, Franklin's talent flowered into a garden of masterpieces gaily tinted with his splendid humor.

One of the earliest of these was written in response to the growing British custom of deporting its convicts to the colonies. It had reached the point where "exportation" rather than "deportation" described this deplorable action. England offhandedly asserted that it aimed at the improvement of the colonies. However, the American recipients of the mother country's gift couldn't see things quite in that light. Most of the felons were at best dangerous and disruptive, seeing their transfer as an opportunity to practice their obnoxious trades on new soil.

Franklin therefore proposed in a newspaper piece that the colonies repay England's benevolence by exporting our native rattlesnake for distribution in the parks and gardens of London. With a straight face, he suggested that the problems of snakes could be handled by the English as easily as Americans were handling the problems of convicts—which was to imply, not at all. "May not the honest, rough British gentry, by a familiarity with these reptiles, learn to creep and to insinuate and to slaver and to wriggle into place (and perhaps to poison such as stand in their way): qualities of no small advantage to courtiers?" Franklin asked. Unfortunately, the satire brought about more American laughter than British reform.

He turned to other animal imagery to demonstrate

displeasure with the English, whose government of the colonies was beginning to show less and less appreciation of their needs. Relying on the folk wisdom he had put together in the *Almanac*, he used the device of the fable to warn the mother country that in exploiting the resources and good nature of the colonies and their inhabitants, it might be taking on a tougher opponent than it thought. "An eagle, king of birds," went one of these fables, "saw a cat basking in the sun, mistook it for a rabbit, stooped, seized it, and carried it up into the air, intending to prey on it. The cat, turning, set her claws into the eagle's breast; who, finding his mistake, opened his talons and would have let her drop; but Puss, unwilling to fall so far, held faster; and the eagle, to get rid of this inconvenience, found it necessary to set her down where he took her up."

Another was even more pointed: "A herd of cows had long afforded plenty of milk, butter, and cheese to an avaricious farmer, who grudged them the grass they subsisted on, and at length mowed it to make money of the hay, leaving them to shift as they could, and yet still expected to milk them as before, but the cows, offended with his unreasonableness, resolved for the future to suckle one another."

Franklin in this period felt a growing conviction that only through unity could the colonies counteract an increasingly oppressive British power. Revolution was not to enter his mind until much later, and even then he would greet it with profound misgivings. But he did not consider it revolutionary for the colonies to join hands in a bid for more effective cooperation with—or opposition to—all the countries or peoples they had to deal with including France, England, and the Indians. To illustrate this he printed a cartoon—generally accepted as the first published in America—depicting an eight-piece snake, seven pieces representing a colony each and the eighth, New England. He captioned it "Join or Die."

He supported this dream with a number of sensible proposals, but he was to learn that the world is often governed not by good sense but by power and self-interest. His frustration was increasing in much the same way as that of the colonies was as they knocked against the wall of British exploitiveness. Realizing, therefore, that sense would not play a part in handling the English, he turned to nonsense instead.

By the 1770's the issue was taxation, which Americans, having no representation in the British Parliament, regarded as more of a demand for tribute than a fair levy. The English rationalized these imposts to themselves and their subjects in many ways, but no matter how they explained it, it still came out "tribute" to the colonists. Franklin was in England at the time, officially representing some of the colonies but unofficially speaking for all of them, and in 1773 he devised a jolly good hoax on his host country. Remembering that England had once, after the Saxon invasion many centuries earlier, been a "colony" of the Germans, he gave the English back "a bit of their own."

He published in a newspaper an ultimatum in the form of an edict signed by "The King of Prussia," Prussia then being more or less synonymous with Germany in those days. This edict, directed to the English people, reminded them that they were still a colony of Germany by virtue of the Saxon occupation, and that they had been shamefully neglecting to pay their tributes to Prussia, the mother country, for some seven or eight centuries. The edict then went on to justify this renewed demand for tribute, and those Englishmen shrewd enough to realize that a joke was being played on them—quite a number took the demands most seriously!—read "England" for Germany, and "America" for England. The edict declared:

> Whereas we ourself [meaning Germany] have in the last war fought and defended the said colonies [meaning England] against the power of France, and thereby enabled them to make conquests from the said power in America, for which we have not yet received adequate compensation; and whereas it is just and expedient that a revenue should be raised from the said colonies in Britain, towards our indemnification; and that those who are descendants of our ancient subjects, and thence still owe us obedience, should contribute to the replenishing of our royal coffers as they must have done had their ancestors remained in the territories now to us appertaining: We do hereby ordain and command. . . .

The King of Prussia went on to ordain and command that all goods imported and exported by England be taxed, that England cease making iron goods and commence shipping the iron to Prussia for manufacture, and that the raising of sheep, except for manure, be discontinued. Finally, the King of Prussia granted clemency to all villains and convicts in German prisons and sent them to Great Britain "for the better peopling of that country"—the same phrase the British had used when sending convicts to America.

Further along in the document the King explained

that since the regulations he was imposing were identical to those which England was imposing on the American colonies, he couldn't imagine England finding them unfair. Somehow many Englishmen found them quite unfair anyway—but not enough to withdraw the very same ones they were pressing upon Americans.

Around the same time Franklin published his "Rules by Which a Great Empire May Be Reduced to a Small One," which, together with the "Edict by the King of Prussia," stands as the foremost satirical work written by an American before the nineteenth century. In this essay he advised, once again in a perfectly serious manner, the ministers of the British government on the best way to ruin their country's relations with a colony. No *particular* colony was specified; Franklin was merely suggesting that if there were a colony around that Britain wanted to ruin, here were twenty ways to do it. These ways, it will come as no surprise, were identical to those that England had used to erode its relations with the colonies in America. Treat them with suspicion, Franklin suggested; send stupid, greedy men to govern them; burden them with taxes; reject their petitions; deprive them of their freedom; scorn their rights; send armies into their towns.

Article XV, for example, exhorted the naval ministry to convert honest officers of the British navy into miserable colonial customs officers:

> Let those who in time of war fought gallantly in defence of their countrymen, in peace be taught to prey upon them. Let them learn to be corrupted by . . . smugglers; but (to show their diligence) scour with armed boats every bay, harbour, river, creek, cove, or nook throughout the coast of

> your colonies; stop and detain every coaster, every wood-boat, every fisherman; tumble their cargoes and even their ballast inside out and upside down; and if a penn'orth of pins is found unentered, let the whole be seized and confiscated. Thus shall the trade of your colonists suffer more from their friends in time of peace than it did from their enemies in war.

But however brilliant they were, his efforts, like those of the land he spoke for, failed to relieve the abuses committed by the British. If there had ever been a chance to prevent the colonies from exerting force to gain satisfaction, it was lost forever when the more radical elements gained control of America's patriotic movement and began pushing it towards war. Although many conservatives recoiled from such extremes, the course soon appeared inescapable.

Right up to the last, Franklin worked towards reconciliation, applying humor as a means of reducing the pressures of antagonism. But while the Continental Congress was convening in Philadelphia, hostilities were breaking out in Lexington, Massachusetts: the dissolution of ties between the mother country and her daughter had already begun. To his English friend Edmund Burke, who had spoken out bravely in Parliament in favor of conciliation, Franklin wrote a capricious account of these first moments: "You will see by the papers that General Gage called his Assembly together to propose Lord North's pacific plan; but before they could meet, [Gage] drew the sword and began the war. His troops made a most vigorous retreat—twenty miles in three hours—scarce to be paralleled in history; the feeble Americans, who pelted them all the way, could

Even after Lexington and Concord, Franklin maintained his sense of humor despite the grim-looking future.

scarce keep up with them." It would appear that Franklin could not take the skirmish seriously. Perhaps he could not yet grasp the enormity of war between Britain and America. More likely, shrewd man that he was, he wanted to play up the ridiculousness of it, keeping the tone light in the hope that both parties would realize before it was too late that someone could get *hurt* with the firearms they were aiming at each other.

Even after Lexington and Concord Franklin did everything possible to bring about a truce. Lord Howe of England proposed that the Americans and British meet to settle their differences before a decisive blow was struck for either side. Franklin and John Adams agreed to meet Howe and, under a white flag, made for a rendezvous in Staten Island. The two Americans, trying to appear as if they were playing the game from a position of power, would not accept Howe's prediction that if the war went to a conclusion America would be defeated. Franklin was in fine fettle that day, and when Howe said he would mourn deeply if America fell, Franklin, a master of the double meaning, said, "My lord, we will use our utmost endeavors to save your lordship that mortification."

The meetings with Howe did not, of course, end in reconciliation, and the nations plunged into a war to the finish.

The Revolution was a time of great solemnity for the colonies. Except for the usual coarse jokes of the soldier there is not much in the way of Revolutionary humor to be found. The stakes were too high, the struggle too bitter, and the losses too severe. Nevertheless, Benjamin Franklin tried to keep his spirits and everyone else's up, and a number of examples of his irrepressible wit are available to us today. Most famous of all—though some historians believe it to be apocryphal—is the remark he made after helping draft the Declaration of Independence. Upon putting his famous signature to the bottom of it, John Hancock declared sternly, "We must be unanimous; there must be no pulling different ways; we must all hang together." To which Franklin rejoined: "Yes, we must indeed all hang together, or most assuredly we shall all hang separately."

Though seventy years old, the indispensable Franklin was dispatched to France to negotiate loans and raise sympathy for the American cause. In Paris he made his greatest triumph yet, hailed as the very model of a Noble Savage, a backwoods Voltaire with coonskin cap and spectacles. The French considered him the personification of the majestic New World innocent grappling heroically with Old World decadence.

Although the notion of the Noble Savage was expressed by the French philosopher and contemporary of Franklin's, Jean-Jacques Rousseau, the idea existed in the European mind long before Rousseau stated it. Imbedded deeply in the Old World consciousness was the belief that America was a land where innocence could be regained, and any product of the American experience would emerge pure and incorruptible. Thus the French were prepared to endow Franklin with these qualities even if he had not been endowed with them himself. Luckily Franklin did actually possess an element of goodness and dignity pure and irreducible; the role of Noble Savage was not the kind a man could fake among the sharp-eyed courtiers of Paris.

At the same time, he had lived too long, had struck too many compromises, was too much a product of Europe to be as innocent as Europeans made him out to be. But he knew perfectly well that by acting out the part that Europe wanted so anxiously to see performed, he could wring out of its coffers the wherewithal to rescue his impecunious country. And so he played his part consummately, capitalizing on this strange kind of hero worship to rally the French—and many liberal Englishmen as well—overwhelmingly to his support and the support of his country. It is no exaggeration to say that no campaign of the Revolutionary War achieved more than the one that Ben Franklin, armed only with his charm, wit, and experience, waged in the salons of Paris. Indeed, the crucial campaigns that won the war for the Revolutionists might have collapsed altogether had they not been financed by cash raised by the aged Philadelphian across the sea.

Franklin was to live for another decade, to bear witness happily to the forging of our mighty Constitution, but it is appropriate that we end this portrait of him with the mission to France. That effort, which summoned all of the wisdom and humor he had accumulated over seventy years of living, can be called the crowning achievement of his life. For by using France's distorted image of him to gain the country's confidence to the tune of millions of dollars, he brought off the greatest of all his hoaxes, a practical joke whose consequences were virtually earthshaking. In a way, the theme was the same as the one he had stated as a boy in the Dogood papers he slipped under the door of his brother's shop in Boston: that a simple, honest, but shrewd individual could get the best of a bargain with the most civilized of hypocrites. It was a theme we have seen annunciated by Nathaniel Ward; it is the same one we will see again and again as America's humor takes form in the centuries that follow the glorious Revolutionary era of which Franklin was patron saint.

3

The First American Bard

"IN ALL THE FOUR QUARTERS OF THE GLOBE," SNEERED Sydney Smith, an Englishman writing in the early nineteenth century, "who reads an American book?"

The question infuriated American men of letters, not because it was unfair but, quite to the contrary, because they could not come up with a good answer. Oh, we had some good almanacs, some fine histories and nature studies, some excellent collections of sermons and political papers. But were they read abroad? It appears that they were either too provincial to interest foreigners, or the foreigners were too contemptuous of the settlements across the sea—even if those settlements *had* licked the greatest power in Europe—to stoop to read what we claimed were good books. Perhaps they had a point; with

Dryden, Pope, Swift, Shakespeare, Dante, Voltaire, and Diderot to read, what need had they for the likes of Cotton Mather? Who read American books? Sad to say —only Americans.

The Revolution over and the Constitution enacted into law, the country turned to the task of discovering itself physically and intellectually. Independent at last, America now had a clear-cut chance at speaking out in its own voice. Men to take advantage of that opportunity were not long forthcoming. Unfortunately, talent would tell only half the story; the other half was recognition. Whether we liked it or not, we were writing with an eye on the reception we would get in Europe. It would take men of superior ability to storm the bastions of European snobbery, bastions built on two thousand years of rich culture, ten times as many years as our country had been settled. It would take men of superior courage too. Just as we had had to resort to force of arms to prove to Europe that we meant business, we would now have to force upon Europe the vitality of our literature.

The man to do the job had been born in New York City in 1783, which was symbolic, for that was the year America won the War of Independence. His name was Washington Irving, a frail but life-loving man possessed of two qualities that no American writer before him had had sufficiently to recommend him to stubborn European tastes. The first was a romantic sense of history, and the second was an elegant style.

Irving did not undergo formal schooling as his older brothers had done, but read hungrily both in the classics and the contemporary work of Continentals. The power and romance of the former merged with the grace and wit of the latter to engrave deep impressions in his receptive mind. Add to these the discipline instilled in him by the study of law, which his father imposed to prevent him from becoming a ne'er-do-well.

He first tried his literary wings with some whimsical satires on New York affairs. Early in his twenties he traveled, visiting first the Hudson River sites that were to provide the scenes for his most important American works, and then Europe where the depth and color of history stirred him profoundly. A year after returning to the United States he collaborated with his brother William and James K. Paulding on a series of essays which once again looked to Addison for their inspiration. They took aim at the follies of fashion, politics, and business, attempting to be instructive, entertaining, and moralistic at one and the same time. These occasional essays went under the title *Salmagundi*, a kind of literary smorgasbord consisting both of delicacies and table scraps. These were as avidly read as *The New Yorker*'s "Talk of the Town" columns are read today.

But it wasn't until his mid-twenties that he brought forth the book that was to establish his reputation as the first man of American belles-lettres. It started out merely as a humorous history of New York, begun in answer to a stuffy guide to the city written by Samuel Mitchell. It was not long, however, before Irving saw greater potential in his work than a mere parody. The history of New York was packed with the elements of an epic; not a serious epic such as Homer's song of the siege of Troy, but rather a tongue-in-cheek one. He would employ the style known as mock-heroic, elevating fools to the stature of heroes in order to deflate their pomposities.

Though aware of the grandiosity of the scheme, Irving could not see that he was going far beyond the historical, far beyond the mock-heroic. What he was drawing a bead on was the most important idea in American life, an idea we have come to call The American Dream. The dream was very much the same thing Europeans thought of when they talked about the Noble Savage of the New World: the dream was an opportunity for a new start, for rediscovery of innocence, for a life unencumbered by the weight of Old World history and tradition, for a casting away of the corruptions and sins of a decadent culture. Motivated by the magic lure of this dream, and by its sister-dream of discovering untold riches in the American wilderness, Europeans had migrated to our shores in enormous numbers.

Needless to say, what they found here, though new and exciting and challenging, could not possibly have filled such a large order. Many did discover themselves and regain innocence, and many did make their fortunes here. But for most immigrants disillusionment was inevitable; the reality just could not have lived up to such high expectations. America was the Land of Opportunity, true, but the men who settled in it were no different from men of any other time or place: human nature was human nature, and much of it was far from divine. If environment were everything, America would have been paradise on earth, but what men carried to this land in their hearts compared poorly with the sublimity of our lakes, forests, and valleys. An unrepentant soul could not find redemption in a thousand paradises.

But out of this disillusionment was born a uniquely American way of looking at life. It was a kind of irony, a contrast between what one hoped for and what one got.

A HISTORY

OF

NEW YORK,

FROM THE BEGINNING OF THE WORLD TO THE END OF THE DUTCH DYNASTY.

CONTAINING

Among many Surprising and Curious Matters, the Unutterable Ponderings of WALTER THE DOUBTER, the Disastrous Projects of WILLIAM THE TESTY, and the Chivalric Achievments of PETER THE HEADSTRONG, the three Dutch Governors of NEW AMSTERDAM; being the only Authentic History of the Times that ever hath been, or ever will be Published.

BY DIEDRICH KNICKERBOCKER.

De waarheid die in duister lag,
Die komt met klaarheid aan den dag.

IN TWO VOLUMES.

VOL. II.

PUBLISHED BY INSKEEP & BRADFORD, NEW YORK, BRADFORD & INSKEEP, PHILADELPHIA; WM. M'ILHENNEY, BOSTON; COALE & THOMAS, BALTIMORE; AND MORFORD, WILLINGTON, & CO. CHARLESTON.

....

1809.

The title page of Knickerbocker's A History of New York.

This irony is the core of the American sense of humor. If one saw life pessimistically, his humor was bitter, if optimistically he reacted benignly. We will see examples of both kinds of humor as, from this period in American history, we watch the American dream restated again and again and then see the American reality contrasted with it. Happily, Washington Irving was a good-natured soul whose view of American history was gentle and benevolent.

The hoax with which Irving put his *A History of New York* over on the public was worthy of the best gimmicks used today. He pretended that the manuscript had been left behind by one Diedrich Knickerbocker in a rooming house, and that he, Irving, had arranged for it to be printed to compensate the owner of the house for the rent that Knickerbocker owed. In this way Irving wove an enchanting, tantalizing tale around the origins of the work, and made them even more appetizing by inserting "teasers" in the newspaper to stimulate curiosity about the forthcoming book. All of these tactics may have been unnecessary, though, for it was received so enthusiastically that it might not have made much difference had Irving published it straightforwardly under his own name.

The book follows the events of the establishment of New Amsterdam: from exploration of the territory by Hudson, through settlement by Dutch explorers and merchants, and on to the ascendancy of Peter Stuyvesant and his ill-fated struggle with the English. Irving found the Dutch delicious targets for satire, and from the first he prodded their soft spots, describing their sailors as a most lubberly lot who "ate hugely, drank profusely, and slept immeasurably." With men like these for a crew, it was a miracle that Hudson's *Half-Moon* reached America at all.

As the book goes on, however, the reader begins to realize that Irving is not merely making light of the Dutch: he is using them as symbols of his contemporaries. Anyone of Irving's day reading Knickerbocker's account of how the Dutch exploited the Indians, for example, was aware that such exploitation was being carried out at that very moment:

> A boat was immediately despatched to enter into a treaty with [the Indians], and approaching the shore, hailed them through a trumpet, in the most friendly terms; but so horribly confounded were these poor savages at the tremendous and uncouth sound of the Low-Dutch language, that they one and all took to their heels, and scampered over the Bergen hills; nor did they stop until they had buried themselves, head and ears, in the marshes on the other side, where they all miserably perished to a man. . . .

After conquest by arms, the second stage of exploitation was through trade, and the Dutch masterfully manipulated the Indians in bargaining:

> A brisk trade for furs was soon opened; the Dutch traders were scrupulously honest in their dealings, and purchased by weight, establishing it as an invariable table of avoirdupois, that the hand of a Dutchman weighed one pound, and his foot two pounds. It is true, the simple Indians were often puzzled by the great disproportion between bulk and weight, for let them place a bundle of furs, never so large, in one scale, and a Dutchman put his hand or foot in the other, the bundle was sure to kick the beam;—never was a package of furs known to weigh more than two pounds in the market of Communipaw!

"Dutch Weight," an engraving from one edition of A History of New York.

Finally, the Indians were cheated out of their land. Here Irving uncorked a roundhouse swipe at land speculators, the unscrupulous sharps who grabbed land in any way they could and resold it for fantastically high prices. The practice was widespread in Irving's time, but it could be expected that it would grow even more virulent as men moved into the limitless land of Louisiana recently purchased by President Jefferson from France.

For some time the Dutch colony prospered, but happy times were not to last much longer, for it found itself slowly surrounded and preyed on by a particularly aggressive and unpleasant breed: the Yankee. Though we think of Yankees today simply as American northerners, in Irving's day the word had a special meaning. They were a tribe of lean, shrewd, tough New Englanders of English origin, aggressive settlers and brilliant, often unscrupulous, traders. And while these traits imparted great strength to the American character, they still compared most unfavorably with the virtues of the Puritans from whom they were descended. When foreign people today refer to Yankee imperialism, it is with that image in mind that they speak.

Irving found the Yankees good material for satire. In spite of the persecutions their ancestors had suffered in the mother country, these descendants of the faith of Oliver Cromwell had grown at least as intolerant as their former oppressors. Using that intolerance as a springboard, Irving attacked the wave of bigotry that seemed to be carrying his contemporaries away in reaction to the break with England. Thirty-five years after revolting against the abuses perpetrated by the British—abuses listed in the Declaration of Independence—Americans were now flagrantly committing them. "Have we not," Irving cried out, departing from the light tone of the book, "within but a few years released ourselves from the shackles of government which cruelly denied us the privilege of governing ourselves, and using in full latitude that invaluable member, the tongue? and are we not at this very moment striving our best to tyrannize over the opinions, tie up the tongues, and ruin the fortunes of one another?"

These lusty Yankees edged closer and closer to the outskirts of Dutch property, and before long were infiltrating the lands that the Dutch had struggled so hard to cheat the Indians out of. These inroads by the so-called Yankee squatters—people who settled illegally on land in the hopes of making their claims good later on—marked the beginning of the struggle for possession of the Hudson River valley and the growing city at the mouth of it. The situation grew critical, but once again the pipe-puffing city council, governed by Wouter Van Twiller, couldn't make up its mind to take decisive action. "There are certain emergencies," Irving lamented, "when your profound legislators and sage deliberative councils are mightily in the way of a nation, and when an ounce of hare-brained decision is worth a pound of sage doubt and cautious discussion."

But the sage and cautious council did nothing, hoping the threat would simply go away, and so it was not long before the Yankees were overrunning the Dutch settlements, exhibiting that turbulent restlessness and half-lawless ambitiousness that characterized the frontier. "In truth," said Irving, "they are a wonderful and all-prevalent people, of that class who only require an inch to gain an ell, or a halter to gain a horse. From the time they first gained a foothold on Plymouth Rock, they began to migrate, progressing and progressing from place to place, and from land to land, making a little here and a little there, and controverting the old proverb, that a rolling stone gathers no moss. Hence they have facetiously received the nickname of THE PILGRIMS: that is to say, a people who are always seeking a better country than their own."

Luckily, around the time that the Dutch-Yankee conflict reached a crisis, Peter Stuyvesant, a wooden-legged tyrant of stupendous ability, came to power in New Amsterdam and began wielding his authority like a mighty sword, slicing through the poky transactions of the city council with broad swipes of common sense, and executing decisions with ferocious willfulness. It was vital that the townspeople be organized and defenses erected. The British were backing the Yankee claims and would no doubt be assembling an expedition to enforce them.

Stuyvesant went to Boston to treat with the Yankees in their own stronghold, and while he was away the Dutch citizens rallied to defend their city, arming themselves with every weapon they could find. With no English army in sight it was rather easy for the burghers to be excessively brave. Irving describes how the orators and politicians repaired to their popular assemblies,

> striving who should bawl loudest, and exceed the others in hyperbolical bursts of patriotism, and in resolutions to uphold and defend the government. In these sage meetings it was resolved that they were the most enlightened, the most dignified, the most formidable, and the most ancient community upon the face of the earth. This resolution being carried unanimously, another was immediately proposed—whether it were not possible and politic to exterminate Great Britain? upon which sixty-nine members spoke in the affirmative, and only one arose to suggest some doubts, who as a punishment for treasonable presumption, was immediately seized by the mob, and tarred and feathered. . . .

Naturally, when it came down to cases, the puffed-up courage of the burghers rushed out like air from a deflating balloon. As the news reached them of the approaching English troops, they tried to determine upon a course of action, but could accomplish nothing because it meant spending money. If they raised an army it would amount to feeding a horde of locusts; if they fit out a navy they would merely be throwing their money into the sea; and to build fortifications was to bury their money in the earth. "A kick left no scar," they concluded; "a broken head cured itself; but an empty purse was of all maladies the slowest to heal, and one in which nature did nothing for the patient." They determined to let the English conquer them, and by the time the enraged Stuyvesant returned it was too late. Realizing he could not overcome the apathy and niggardliness of his townspeople, he sadly turned his city over to the British forces, who renamed it for their patron the Duke of York.

Diedrich Knickerbocker's *A History of New York*, though readable on one level as humorous history, is also obviously an allegory, a story that represents another story. It can, in other words, be read as Irving's view of his nation as it had turned out since the days of Dutch and Puritan settlers. What was that view?

It was that in some ways the original vision of our forefathers had been corrupted, and a danger existed that it would be further corrupted. He saw, for example, that after our explosion of patriotic effort during the Revolutionary War and establishment of the Constitution, apathy and indifference had set into the American soul. The young nation had isolated itself and turned inward, reviling its European origins and shunning much of the responsibility of government by the people. Too many individuals were leaving that responsibility to their elected representatives, resulting in a kind of moral flabbiness that left us vulnerable to attack by more aggressive nations. At the same time, our elected representatives either could not or would not act; the trouble with committees, councils, and legislatures was that they made decisions with ponderous slowness, and acted on those decisions no more quickly. We had not yet learned how to coordinate the executive and legislative branches of government, and Irving was illustrating a potentially fatal flaw in the government we had chosen for ourselves. Though no one really wanted a king, not a few people longed for some kind of ruler who, by his solitary decision, could place his government quickly and conclusively into motion. In other words, we must beware of bogging down into complacency on the one hand, or choosing despotic leaders on the other.

What could better illustrate Irving's fears than the near-disaster of our War of 1812, but a few years after publication of the Knickerbocker history? Here is an account of the burning of Washington by an English officer that sounds all too disturbingly like Irving's rendering of the behavior of the burghers:

> So confident had they been of the success of their troops, that few of them had dreamt of quitting their houses, or abandoning the city; nor was it till the fugitives from the battle began to rush in, filling every place as they came with dismay, that the President himself thought of providing for his safety. That gentleman, as I was credibly informed, had gone forth in the morning with the army, and had continued

among his troops till the British forces began to make their appearance. Whether the sight of his enemies cooled his courage or not, I cannot say, but, according to my informer, no sooner was the glittering of our arms discernible, than he began to discover that his presence was more wanted in the senate than with the army. . . . He hurried back to his own house, that he might prepare a feast for the entertainment of his officers, when they should return victorious. For the truth of these details, I will not be answerable; but this much I know, that the feast was actually prepared, though, instead of being devoured by American officers, it went to satisfy the less delicate appetites of a party of English soliders.

On April 23, 1813, Henry Brevoort received a letter from a Scottish friend of his concerning Diedrich Knickerbocker's history, which Brevoort had presented to him. The Scotsman owned:

I have never read anything so closely resembling the style of Dean [Jonathan] Swift as the annals of Diedrich Knickerbocker. I have been employed these few evenings in reading them aloud to Mrs. S. and two ladies who are our guests, and our sides have been absolutely sore with laughing. I think too there are passages which indicate that the author possesses powers of a different kind, and has some touches which remind me of Sterne. I beg you will have the kindness to let me know when Mr. Irving takes pen in hand again, for assuredly I shall expect a very great treat. . . .

The letter was signed by the great poet and novelist Walter Scott.

Six years later Scott was to help Irving get his *Sketch Book*, a collection of observations and stories including "The Legend of Sleepy Hollow" and "Rip Van Winkle," published in England. It was this volume that established Irving as the first notable man of letters the new nation had produced. Perhaps its warm reception was due to the essay in it entitled "English Writers of America," in which he called for an end to the senseless quarrel between the two cultures over the value of American literature. Americans, he said, were becoming too adult to maintain feelings of inferiority, while the English were too compassionate to keep up their snobbish, indiscriminate contempt of all things American. "Is this golden band of kindred sympathies, so rare between nations, to be broken forever?" he asked plaintively. The golden band, at that depressed moment in the Anglo-American relations following the War of 1812, had been reduced to but a few threads; but among them were the books of Washington Irving.

"In all the four quarters of the globe," Sydney Smith had asked, "who reads an American book?" Walter Scott, then one of the most glamorous, popular, and influential writers in the English language, proudly answered "*I* do." And before long, many more Englishmen were to add their affirmations to his.

4

The Brahmins

BY THE MID-1820'S, ALMOST TWO GENERATIONS AFTER OUR Founding Fathers threw down the gauntlet of defiance before the English, the eastern tidewater was no longer a series of rough-hewn communities strung tenuously together, vulnerable to foreign armies, domestic savages, and internal discords. Its important cities, though still small by present standards, had grown to respectable size. Their institutions and systems—colleges, militia, fire brigades, sanitation facilities, and the like—had begun to take on a semblance of organization. Trade was thriving, so that communities that had struggled desperately for basic goods could feel they could take certain supplies for granted. Men were tearing down log structures and rebuilding them with stone and mortar. Luxuries like silk and wine were displayed more commonly. In short, the people of the East started to regard their nation's existence as a fact to be counted on, a fact with an inspiring past and a substantial future.

The East had passed a milestone. It no longer existed on a raw survival basis. As a result, men could turn their conversation from immediate problems to more abstract ideas. Conditions were ripening for the emergence of imaginative literature, the kind not immediately aimed at instructing in the manner of the Puritan ministers, or dealing pragmatically with political, economic, or scientific questions in the manner of Benjamin Franklin. No one, fifty or a hundred years earlier, could have written as Emerson now wrote: "If eyes were made for seeing, Then Beauty is its own excuse for being." Americans did not have, until the nineteenth century, time to create beauty for its own sake. Washington Irving had been the first American writer to earn a living from his pen alone, but many were now to follow.

While the East was beginning to settle down, however, the West was disclosing vistas and opportunities wilder than anything eighteenth-century Americans had imagined possible. The Louisiana Purchase had doubled the nation's area, and settlers were rushing in to populate it. It began to dawn on Easterners that the opening of the western frontier might prove crucial to our development. But they never expected that dawn to burst upon them as suddenly as it did as, in 1828, a Westerner—and Tennessee, where he had grown up, was the West in those days—was elected President of the United States.

Suddenly, as Andrew Jackson's cronies swaggered through the White House for the inauguration festivities, stood on damask chairs in their muddy boots, brawled, drank, swore, and smashed china, Americans saw the logical consequence of their credo that all men were created equal. After six Presidents, from Washington to John Quincy Adams, more or less in the aristocratic mold, the common man had arrived. And not a few people shuddered. Compare our dream of a legislature peopled by august patriots, with this description written not long after the Jackson administration by a horrified lady observer:

> It is somewhat remarkable too, at first, to say the least, to see so many honorable members with swelled faces; and it is scarcely less remarkable to discover that this appearance is caused by the quantity of tobacco they contrive to stow within the hollow of the cheek. It is strange enough, too, to see an honorable gentleman leaning back in his tilted chair, with his legs on the desk before him, shaping a convenient "plug" with his penknife, and when it is quite ready for use, shooting the old one from his mouth as from a pop-gun, and clapping the new one in its place.
>
> I was surprised to observe that even steady old chewers of great experience are not always good marksmen, which has rather inclined me to doubt that general proficiency with the rifle, of which we have heard so much in England. Several gentlemen called upon me who, in the course of conversation, frequently missed the spittoon at five paces; and one . . . mistook the closed sash for the open window at three.

A division in American life and thought was becoming apparent, a division you could almost trace physically by the mere act of running your finger down the spine of the Appalachian mountain range. On the eastern side of it, men were building a solid empire on the foundations laid by pilgrims and pioneers. There the bond with England and the European continent was still strong; a good road system linked city and city, state and state; the tradition of learning ran like a deep grain through the eastern fiber.

But on the western side, men were venturing into the wilderness where there was no road system but animal paths and river courses, no tradition but survival of the fittest, no political order except aristocracy of the tough, and where learning was nearly valueless save for the reading of clouds, spoor, and smoke signals. Under these circumstances a much different kind of democracy had to develop than the eastern kind, which depended so heavily on reason.

So fierce was Western democracy that Westerners began characterizing their Eastern brethren as aristocratic snobs. The image was not entirely inaccurate by any means. Easterners felt they were carrying the torch of civilization above the rabble of ill-bred, unmannerly Westerners. The cultured men of the seaboard were frightened that the Western influence, especially in the seat wherein resided the highest power in the land, would bring barbarism to the new continent. If, then, they could not have enlightened, cultured men of reason in the White House, they would establish an unofficial aristocracy, based on creative intelligence, outside of it. Taste can be as tyrannical a ruler as any sceptered despot, and as forces began lining up, it looked as if the East-West antagonism was to be a matter of good taste versus bad.

Some thought that New York would become the capital city of American taste. Washington Irving dominated our letters for the first quarter of the nineteenth century, so much so that the group of New York-oriented journalists he fathered were called the Knickerbocker School. But even as that generation was filling the city's newspapers with clever if unmemorable verses and essays, the focus of energy was shifting away from Manhattan. It would not return until, a century later, the offices of *The New Yorker* bulged with the talent of a score of incomparable wits.

Boston, on the other hand, had been an intellectual center from the outset. The high educational standards of the Puritan ministry had made the Bay Colony a fortress of religious and political thought. Harvard, America's first college, had been founded there in the 1630's, and two centuries later was in the vanguard of a rebellion against the restrictions of Puritan doctrine. Unitarians, led by William Ellery Channing, rejected the notion that men were born sinners and that their iniquities were passed from father to son forever. This new generation of intellectuals, like the new generations of Americans generally, were convinced that man could develop and better himself in this world, and perhaps find redemption here on earth.

The city had a rich tradition of patriotism: a roll call of America's early political leaders is studded with Bostonians.

Now, in the second quarter of the nineteenth century, the energy that had gone into political and religious revolution was shifting to a literary one, and the generation of poets, writers, thinkers, and scholars who flocked to its banner constituted the most brilliant group of intellectuals assembled since London's Literary Club. Ralph Waldo Emerson, Henry David Thoreau, Nathaniel

Longfellow in his Brahmin study was far removed from the real frontier.

Hawthorne, William Cullen Bryant, Henry Wadsworth Longfellow, John Greenleaf Whittier, James Fenimore Cooper, Oliver Wendell Holmes, William Ellery Channing, James Russell Lowell, Emily Dickinson, and a small army of lesser but still dazzling lights illuminated the American experience.

It was Oliver Wendell Holmes who gave the movement its name. "There is nothing in New England corresponding at all to the feudal aristocracies of the Old World," he admitted. "There is, however, in New England an aristocracy, if you choose to call it so, which has a far greater character of permanence. It has grown to be a *caste*—not in any odious sense—but, by the repetition of the same influences, generation after generation, it has acquired a distinct organization and physiognomy." Holmes styled it "The Brahmin caste of New England."

> There are races of scholars among us, in which aptitude for learning, and all these marks of it I have spoken of, are congenital and hereditary. Their names are always on some college catalogue or other. They break out every generation or two in some learned labor which calls them up after they seem to have died out. At least some newer name takes their place, it may be—but you inquire a little and you find it is the blood of the Edwardses or the Chaunceys or the Ellerys or some of the old historic scholars, disguised under the altered name of a female descendant.

Holmes himself was heir to a heritage of scholarship, his father having been a minister and author, but Oliver was a latecomer to the New England group. Until nearly fifty he contented himself practicing and teaching medicine. But the founding of James Russell Lowell's *Atlantic Monthly* stirred the author secretly lurking in Holmes's breast, and when Lowell invited him to contribute a regular essay to the magazine, he responded with a series of delightful, informal, but extremely urbane chats on subjects sublime and trivial. He called these essays *The Autocrat of the Breakfast Table.*

It was interesting that Holmes called his narrator an "autocrat." It means not merely an aristocrat but an individual vested with absolute power—a kind of despot. It was an unpleasant word to American ears, and even a fighting word to some, for although Holmes's domain was nothing grander than a breakfast table, the idea of such centralized authority was alien to the democratic sentiment governing the American system. But Holmes knew what he was doing: he was intentionally reasserting the aristocratic tradition for the benefit of the western barbarians. "Self-made men?" asked the Autocrat grudgingly; "Well, yes. Of course, everybody likes and respects self-made men. It is a great deal better to be made in that way than not to be made at all. . . . But . . . other things being equal, in most relations of life I prefer a man of family . . . , the man who inherits family traditions and the cumulative humanities of at least four or five generations . . . , the man with the gallery of family portraits."

This kind of talk was poison to the new breed of American who not only had nothing resembling a gallery of family portraits, but was thankful to claim a solid wall to hang them on. What was especially disturbing about this kind of snobbery is that it was hard to distinguish it from the British kind the nation had struggled and shed its blood to escape. As a matter of fact, when you thought about it, you realized that many Americans had turned their eyes back to England, longing for the customs, the depth of history, the established social order that were the glories of that land. England was a country where the common man knew his place.

The New England Brahmins protested vociferously that they were establishing a native American literature, one divorced from English influence. But they rarely departed from English forms and themes, and they were often obsessively concerned with pleasing English critics. Emerson, dean of the New England "school," did speak satirically of the English, as this passage from a sketch shows:

> I have found that Englishmen have such a good opinion of England, that the ordinary phrases in all good society, of postponing or disparaging one's own things in talking with a stranger, are seriously mistaken by them for an insuppressible homage to the merits of their nation; and the New Yorker or Pennsylvanian who modestly laments the disadvantages of a new country, log-huts and savages, is surprised by the instant and unfeigned commiseration of the whole company, who plainly account all the world out of England a heap of rubbish.

But Emerson never went much further than such tender wrist-slaps, because he had his position to maintain among the English intelligentsia, and if he slapped them too harshly he would lose all the esteem in which they held him. It would take a Mark Twain, a generation later, to show the English that a growing body of Americans truly didn't care a rap what the English thought.

What has all this to do with the American sense of humor? It shows that since Americans were still extremely self-conscious before their English peers, the writers of the New England Renaissance tended to take themselves rather seriously as a whole. They were, after all, aristocrats, and aristocrats of every age have too much to lose by laughing at themselves. It is easier to jab at the pompous British aristocrat from underneath, as Franklin had done, than to make wholesome fun of the common man from on high. This freezing-up of the funnybone is a trait that would reappear almost every time America, after a crisis, consolidated itself as a nation.

Thus men like Bryant, Whittier, Longfellow, Emerson, Hawthorne, and Thoreau rarely permitted themselves the release of out-and-out knee-slapping hilarity. They had the dignity of their Establishment to protect, and you can't run a respectable Establishment if the owners are carrying on in an undignified way. There is much wit to be found in the New England Renaissance, to be sure—but it is subdued and erudite, as if professors were exchanging subtle ironies in a college corridor. To hear a haw-haw you had to find a Westerner.

And so the literature of the Brahmins, while it represents the greatest prose and poetic achievements the young nation had brought forth to date, cannot be characterized as humorous. "Life is real, life is earnest," Longfellow sang solemnly.

The deepest preoccupation of this group of writers was nature. But because nature was for them an expression of divine order, a means to grace and salvation and self-revelation, it could not be taken as a laughing matter. Sometimes, of course, nature itself smiled, and when it did these poets were quick to smile with it. Even Emerson permitted himself a scandalous cavort from time to time, such as his poetic escapade "The Humble-Bee," the first stanza of which goes:

Burly, dozing Humble-bee
Where thou art is clime for me,
Let them sail for Porto Rique,
Far-off heats through seas to seek;
I will follow thee alone,
Thou animated torrid-zone!
Zigzag steerer, desert cheerer,
Let me chase thy waving lines;

> *Keep me nearer, me thy hearer,*
> *Singing over shrubs and vines.*

And Thoreau, a bit more down-to-earth than most of his friends and colleagues, diverted himself on Walden Pond with a hide-and-seek caper with a loon:

> It was a pretty game, played on the smooth surface of the pond, a man against a loon. Suddenly your adversary's checker disappears beneath the board, and the problem is to place yours nearest to where his will appear again. Sometimes he would come up unexpectedly on the opposite side of me, having apparently passed directly under the boat. So long-winded was he and so unweariable, that when he had swum furthest he would immediately plunge again, nevertheless; and then no wit could divine where in the deep pond, beneath the smooth surface, he might be speeding his way like a fish, for he had time and ability to visit the bottom of the pond in its deepest part. . . . How surprised must the fishes be to see this ungainly visitor from another sphere speeding his way amid their schools. . . . I found that it was as well for me to rest on my oars and wait for his reappearing as to endeavor to calculate where he would rise; for again and again, when I was straining my eyes over the surface one way, I would suddenly be startled by his unearthly laugh behind me.

There was one Brahmin, however, with a broader sense of humor than the others. Though a man of profound learning and critical acumen, James Russell Lowell was more able than most of his contemporaries to let his long hair down. He could write in the dialect of the common man, and was not afraid to poke fun at anyone deserving it. He was actually the only writer of the lot who could step away from himself and find himself rather ridiculous.

It often follows that if a man can find himself funny he can find just about anything else funny as well. Lowell surveyed his colleagues of New England and decided that the lot of them were singularly lacking in levity. And so in 1848 he had published his *Fable for Critics*, a poetic satire that held uncomfortably close to the burning coals all of the important writers of his time—not excluding himself. The result was the best thing of its kind since Pope's *Dunciad*—and much funnier than that often vicious lampoon.

In portraying Emerson, for example, Lowell chose to make fun of the man's almost inhuman severity, a dignity so unapproachable that he reminded one of a bronze deity sequestered in an Oriental shrine. Emerson was as close to the embodiment of pure thought as anyone Lowell could think of; in fact he was so intellectual that Lowell wondered if Emerson's universe were not more a creation of Emerson than of the Almighty:

For though he builds glorious temples, 'tis odd
He leaves never a doorway to get in a god.
'Tis refreshing to old-fashioned people like me
To meet such a primitive Pagan as he,
In whose mind all creation is duly respected
As parts of himself—just a little projected. . . .

Lowell likened William Cullen Bryant to ice:

There is Bryant, as quiet, as cool, and as dignified,
As a smooth, silent iceberg, that never is
ignified. . . .
Unqualified merits, I'll grant, if you choose, he has
'em,
But he lacks the one merit of kindling enthusiasm;

If he stir you at all, it is just, on my soul,
Like being stirred up with the very North Pole.

James Fenimore Cooper, creator of the Deerslayer and Leatherstocking tales, Lowell mildly teased—though Mark Twain later on was not to show anywhere near as much patience with that somewhat sloppy craftsman:

He has drawn you one character, though, that is new,
One wildflower he's plucked that is wet with the dew
Of this fresh Western world, and, the thing not to
mince,
He has done naught but copy it ill ever since;
His Indians, with proper respect be it said,
Are just Natty Bumpo, daubed over with red,
And his very Long Toms are the same useful Nat,
Rigged up in duck pants and a sou'-wester hat. . . .
And the women he draws from one model don't vary,
As sappy as maples and flat as a prairie.

Lowell saved himself for last, and his self-portrait, of a man who just couldn't remain uninvolved with causes such as abolition, was just as unsparing as those he had painted of the other Brahmins:

There is Lowell, who's striving Parnassus to climb
With a whole bale of isms *tied together with rhyme,*
He might get on alone, spite of brambles and
boulders,
But he can't with that bundle he has on his shoulders,
The top of the hill he will ne'er come nigh reaching
Till he learns the distinction 'twixt singing and
preaching;
His lyre has some chords that would ring pretty well,

But he'd rather by half make a drum of the shell,
And rattle away till he's old as Methusalem,
At the head of a march to the last new Jerusalem.

The strait-laced Brahmins must have smiled stiffly to behold themselves held up to such ridicule, however tender; but those who read *A Fable for Critics* on the western frontier undoubtedly whooped with uncontrollable mirth. Lowell had played as good a practical joke on his own kind as any backwoodsman could play on a dude. Perhaps the poem was a kind of signal for a Western anti-intellectual uprising, for in the 1840's the literary initiative was yanked rudely out of Eastern hands. The Brahmins were left clinging earnestly to their dignity while a brigade of first-rate Western wits joyously kicked the American dream all over the prairies.

5

The Western Clowns

EVERYONE IN AMERICA KNEW THAT THE WEST WAS WHERE IT was happening, to use the modern phrase. Ever since Lewis and Clarke had reported to their President on their breathtaking search for a northwest passage, many Americans had come to look to the land beyond the sunset as a fulfillment of the dream—a fulfillment that had eluded them on the already crowded eastern seaboard. Francis Parkman, one of our first important historians, published stimulating accounts of the West in his *The California and Oregon Trail* and *The Conspiracy of Pontiac.* During his term from 1844 to 1848, President Polk used the stirring phrase "Manifest Destiny" to describe the irresistible movement from eastern shore to western. Trade had long been established on the broad, muddy Mississippi River, but now the River was coming to mean more than a commercial canal. To the romantic men who turned their eyes Pacific-wards, it was a symbol of national expectations.

Every writer of the day, whatever his style or viewpoint, was aware that the presence of the West was affecting his artistic consciousness. Washington Irving, returning from Europe after producing his magnificent books on Spain and Columbus, headed west, a kind of latter-day literary Columbus in search of fabulous lands to write about. Between 1836 and 1838 he produced entertaining and informative chronicles of Western adventurers, the prairies, and of the founding of the Astor empire. Even the Brahmins had to grant that the West was our most promising source of a distinctive national literature. Cooper's tales of backwoodsmen and Indians, however inaccurate and repetitious, were tremendously compelling reading; Longfellow's *Song of Hiawatha*, drawing on lore and legend of Indians on the southern shore of Lake Superior, was to become a kind of poetic national monument; and Lowell, Emerson, Thoreau, Bryant, and Whittier, among others, hailed the wilderness as a paradise where man's innate virtue could flourish.

Of course, had these idealists moved out of their intellectual fortresses and plunged earnestly into the wilderness, they might have had to revise their lofty convictions about the divinity of nature and the essential goodness of man. While Thoreau's adventure on Walden Pond was an inspiring reassertion of those values, it was no genuine test of man against nature. In a way, it was what scientists call a controlled experiment. If the going ever got too rough Thoreau knew he had civilization near at hand. He even confesses that he came out of the woods to dine in town from time to time. That these forays back into "civilization" were "frequently to the detriment of my domestic arrangements" does not alter the fact that Walden was not a fundamental challenge to his survival. He could afford to be benign about man and nature.

But ask a frontiersman about nature and he would tell you of its merciless cruelty; ask him about human goodness and he might reply with something unprintable. In spite of reports filtering back from the frontier about starvation, disease, Indian massacres, and failure of every sort, the dream persisted. The lure of land and freedom, the serene grandeur of nature, the uplifting religiosity of the wild propelled men across the Appalachians.

Some of them were propelled to their dooms, but the hardy survivors emerged deeply changed, their viewpoints on everything completely altered. They had discovered that all their hopes and ideals, including The Dream itself, counted for very little against the awesome laws of nature that prevailed beyond the reaches of Eastern civilization. The realization that whatever we might want out of life, life made its own laws, is one of the essential ingredients in the humor that now came to characterize the West. For in that realization was the germ of all our national distrust and irreverence for the works and ways of man's brain. Charles H. Smith, a popular humorist of the time writing under the name Bill Arp, put it this way in his reply to the faculty of a law school:

> I hav reseved your kind invitashun to address your Law school. In the situashun in which I am situated, it is onpossible for me to go. I wish I could, for I would like to tell you all I know about law bisiness myself, at this place. We

are engaged in manufakturin it by holesale, and atter while it will be retaled out by the lawyers to any body that wants it.

Eastern and foreign observers, travelling through the West, came away with the impression that a carnival was in progress: Americans were laughing at simply everything! On professor, H. H. Boyeson, observed early in the nineteenth century that we "take a facetious view of life and extract the greatest possible amount of amusement out of every situation. It is apt to be one of the first observations of the intelligent foreigner who lands upon our shores, that all things, ourselves included, are with us legitimate subjects for jokes."

Seeking an explanation for this phenomenon, Professor Boyeson put his finger on it when he suggested that "an all-levelling democracy has tended to destroy the sense of reverence which hedges certain subjects with sanctity, guarding them against the shafts of wit." The laughter he was witnessing had been provoked, in other words, by our attitude that nothing in American life was too serious to laugh at.

If one could pinpoint the cause of all this hilarity, it might be the election of Andrew Jackson. What more rollicking prank could be played on the dignified Founding Fathers of the East? Following the very formulas those gentlemen had prescribed in their Constitution, the common man had brought to the highest office in the land a two-fisted whiskey-drinking upstart from Tennessee. After that event, what could be sacred?

The vehicle for Western humor was invariably the newspaper. In a land hungry for communication, the local paper served as a kind of portable cast-iron stove on which everyone in the community could put his feet and exchange information and gossip. The arrival of a printing press from the east usually signified that a town had risen above frontier status and was now, technically at least, settled. Because of the hasty, improvised way these papers were set up, Western writers found them to be like extensions of their verbal spontaneity. David Ross Locke had his *Hancock Jeffersonian*, for instance; Bill Nye his *Laramie Boomerang;* and Charles Farrar Brown his *Cleveland Plain Dealer*.

Because of the sheer grandiosity of the West, the most commonly used literary device was hyperbole—the intentional exaggeration. Characteristic of most of these writers are such images as:

> *A man in Kentucky was so big it took five preachers to preach a sermon over him.*
>
> *An Arkansan was so tall his food froze before it reached his stomach.*
>
> *A Tennessee boy grew so fast he outgrew his clothes before the tailor could finish them.*
>
> *An Illinois woodsman is so lean he has no shadow.*

A good storyteller could develop these pithy expressions into full-blown tales, and it was these "tall stories" that eventually gave rise to the famous legends of the West. T. B. Thorpe's *The Big Bear of Arkansas*, written in 1841, is one of the classics of this form of literature. In Thorpe's description of Arkansas mosquitoes we can see emerging the stuff of which the western tradition is made:

> Well, stranger [says the Hoosier to a companion on a Mississippi riverboat] . . . they are rather *enormous,* and

do push themselves in somewhat troublesome. But, stranger, they never stick twice in the same place; and give them a fair chance for a few months, and you will get as much above noticing them as an alligator. They can't hurt my feelings, for they lay under the skin; and I never knew but one case of injury resulting from them, and that was to a Yankee; and they take worse to foreigners, any how, than they do to natives. But the way they used that fellow up! First they punched him until he swelled up and busted; then he su-per-a-ted, as the doctor called it, until he was as raw as beef.

Obviously, it wasn't far to go from this sort of thing to the heroic exploits of a Paul Bunyan, a Mike Fink, or a Davy Crockett. Here, for example, is a tall tale about Davy Crockett:

Almost every boddy that knows the forrest, understands parfectly well that Davy Crockett never loses powder and ball, havin' ben brort up to blieve it a sin to throw away amminition, and that is the benefit of a vartuous eddikation. I war out in the forrest won arternoon, and had jist got to a plaice called the grate gap, when I seed a rakkoon setting all alone upon a tree. I klapped the breech of Brown Betty to my sholder, and war jist a going to put a piece of led between his sholders, when he lifted one paw, and sez he, "Is your name Crockett?"

Sez I, "You are rite for wonst, my name is Davy Crockett."

"Then," sez he, "you needn't take no further trubble, for I may as well cum down without another word"; and the cretur wauked rite down from the tree, for he considered himself shot.

If Crockett's language seems a bit hard to follow, it is Basic English compared with some of the dialects

Davy Crockett speaking to the rough 'n' ready Westerners.

printed at this time as writer after writer strove both to record accurately the unique accent of his region, and to outdo each other in humorous spelling, pronunciation, and grammar. One of the most capable writers in this vein was George Washington Harris, whose Sut Lovingood is as engaging as any rascal east of the Great Divide. Few could match Sut for his combination of wisdom and linguistic charm, as the following passage on mustaches reveals:

> Mustachus am pow'ful holesum things I speck, tu them what hes the stummick tu wear em. Best buttermilk strainers on yeath. All the scrimpshuns ove butter lodges in the har, an' rubbed in makes it grow, like chicken dung dus inyuns. Strains whisky powerful good, what hes dead flies in hit, an'

then yu kin comb em off ur let em stay, 'cordin tu yer taste. They changes the taste ove a kiss clear over; makes hit tas' an' smell like a mildew'd saddil-blankit, arter hit hed been rid on a sore-back hoss three hundred miles in August, an' increases yer appertite fur sich things 'cordingly. I seed a blue-bird devil a feller onst, all one spring, a-tryin tu git into his mouf tu build a nestes, an' the durn'd fool wer proud ove the bird's preferens, but wudn't let hit git in.

Another well-known writer in the cacographic—a word literally meaning "deformed writing"—style was Josh Billings. Billings, whose real name was Henry Wheeler Shaw, turned to the tradition of proverbial wisdom that Ben Franklin had brought to an art form. In his collection of "affurisms," Billings demonstrated, as Poor Richard had, the wisdom of the humble man. But this humble man had a twang:

If a man haz got 80 thousand dollars at interest, and owns the house he livs in, it aint mutch trouble to be a philosopher.

I suppose that one reason whi the road to ruin iz broad, iz tew accomadate the grate amount of travel in that direkshun.

No man ever yet increased hiz reputashun bi contradikting lies.

Of all Billings' productions, though, the one that has survived longest is his essay "The Mule," which is reproduced here in part:

The mule is haf hoss and haf Jackass, and then comes tu a full stop—natur diskovering her mistake. Tha weigh more akordin to their heft, than enny other kreetur, except a crowbar. Tha kant hear enny quicker, nor further than the hoss, yet their ears are big enuff for snow shoes. You kan trust them with enny one whose life aint worth enny more than the mules. The only wa tu keep them into a paster, is tu turn them into a medder jineing, and let them jump out. Tha are reddy for use, just as soon as they will du tu abuse. Tha haint got enny friends, and will live on huckel berry brush, with an ockasional chance at Kanada Thissels. Tha are a modern invenshun, i don't think the Bible deludes to them at tall. Tha sel for more money than enny other domestick animile. Yu kant tell their age by looking into their mouth, enny more than you kould a Mexican cannons. Tha never have no dissease than a good club wont heal. If tha ever die tha must kum right tu life agin, for i never herd nobody sa "ded mule." Tha are like sum men, very korrupt at harte; ive known them to be good mules for 6 months, just to get a good chanse to kick sumbody.

In these days religion came in for a good ribbing, for in the rough-and-tumble of the wilderness or prairie could be seen a very different Almighty from the increasingly civilized one of the East. The irreverent Westerner did not tiptoe around the sensitive question of man's relations with his Creator. In a chapter from *Some Adventures of Captain Simon Suggs*, Johnson J. Hooper, speaking through the rogue he created, commented on the hypocrisy of some preachers of the day:

Wonder what's the reason these here preachers never hugs up the old ugly women? Never seed one do it in my life—the sperrit never moves 'em that way! It's nater tho'; and the women, *they* never flocks round one o' the old dried-up breethring—bet two to one old splinter-legs thar . . . won't git a chance to say turkey to a good-lookin gall today! Well! who blames 'em? Nater will be nater, all the world over; and I judge ef I was a preacher, I should save the purtiest souls fust, myself!

Superficially, the Westerners' love of bad English, misspellings, and strange pronunciations bespoke their rough quality and their humor. But it went beyond these. It showed, for one thing, that the English language itself, after achieving heights of elegance in the eighteenth century (Dr. Samuel Johnson, it will be recalled, had momentarily fixed the language with his Dictionary), was on the move again, tumbling, twisting, dancing, and cavorting in the mouths of these inelegant people. A new way of speaking was developing in order to express a new way of seeing.

But let no one be fooled. This pretense of semi-literacy disguised a vital wisdom, a wisdom much closer to the idea of the Noble Savage than anything the aristocratic Brahmins of the Eastern establishment had been able to demonstrate. It would not be long before an Eastern magazine declared "New England is no longer king. . . . The South and the West are hereafter to be reckoned upon."

But while the mirth-provoking feud between East and West went on in the 1830's and 1840's, a far more ominous one was growing between North and South, making humorists in every region stop, listen—and frown.

6

Jesters of the Civil War

BY THE LATE 1840'S ALMOST EVERY ASPECT OF AMERICAN thought had begun to revolve around the question of slavery, and like everyone else our humorists began drifting towards one side or another. Like iron filings lining up around the field of a magnet, the hitherto diverse originality of these writers was beginning to line up around two issues: was slavery to be tolerated in a free country? And was it to be extended to the new territories into which Americans were migrating?

The humor of these crucial days is among the best this nation ever produced. For, as often happens, the existence of a single cause gave the writers a clear target to aim at, enabling them to direct their talents more sharply than the random pot-shooting of earlier days.

But there is something sad about the change. The humorist was no longer a simple-hearted passerby, carefreely remarking on whatever tickled his fancy. As in the days of Franklin, he was becoming part politician, employing his genius in the service of a social purpose. However noble the cause of preserving the Union, the humorist who took sides—either with the South or the North—did sacrifice much of his lighthearted innocence. The nation was coming of age, and loss of innocence is the price one pays for it. In the bloody test ahead, hundreds of thousands of gallant men were to pay an even higher price than that.

Slavery had been a concern of Americans for the more than two hundred years since the first Negroes were brought into Virginia. Though no massive opposition had been mounted against the institution, the disturbance of the national conscience over it was always near at hand. It was almost brought into the open at the Constitutional Convention, where Benjamin Franklin questioned the compatibility of our principles with the view that some human beings could be the property of others. But it was such a touchy topic that Franklin did not press it at the Convention. The question went unresolved, and everybody hoped it would settle itself if left alone. But Franklin, typically, brought his humor to bear after his more serious approach failed. He concocted an essay entitled "On the Slave Trade," making believe it was written by an Algerian pirate. These pirates were feared at the time because they preyed on European ships, enslaving the Christians they captured on them. Franklin justified the enslavement of white Christians by Algerians, using exactly the same arguments that America's white Christians were using to explain enslavement of black Africans. By showing slaveowners that fate might one day turn the tables on them, Franklin hoped they would abandon the repellent custom. It was one of his best hoaxes, and as good a piece of antislavery humor as anything that followed. But alas, it failed to affect the question.

On the other hand, Franklin was in good company—for everything else was to fail as well.

In the next century New Englanders picked up the ball, and many Brahmin poets and writers joined the voices of abolitionists William Lloyd Garrison and Henry Ward Beecher in denouncing slavery. Controversy flared over the admission of Texas to the Union, a move bitterly opposed by Northerners fearing the extension of slavery into that territory and its division into five states, throwing the balance of votes in the federal legislature in favor of the South. At last Texas was annexed, but this move signaled war with Mexico.

The war was thought of by many New Englanders as a militaristic attempt by Americans to enlarge the slave area, and it stirred James Russell Lowell, author of *A Fable for Critics*, to raise his pen in protest. The result was a collection of satirical verses he called *The Biglow Papers*, ostensibly written by a patriotic Yankee named Hosea Biglow. The first of these narrated Biglow's encounter with a recruiting sergeant trying to raise troops to fight Mexico. Biglow spoke out against the hypocrisy of so-called liberal Northerners who, claiming to deplore slavery, advocate an oppressive war against a foreign nation:

Want to tackle me *in, du ye?*
I expect you'll hev to wait;
Wen cold lead puts daylight thru ye

You'll begin to kal'late;
S'pose the crows wun't fall to pickin'
All the carkiss from your bones,
Coz you helped to give a lickin'
To them poor half-Spanish drones? . . .

Then, with more than a decade to pass before the rift between North and South grew beyond reconciliation, Lowell sounded this sinister note:

Ef I'd my *way I hed ruther*
We should go to work an' part,
They take one way, we take t'other,
Guess it wouldn't break my heart;
Man hed ough' to put asunder
Them thet God has noways jined;
An' I shouldn't gretly wonder
Ef there's thousands o' my mind.

The American victory over Mexico, coupled with the stampede to California following the discovery of gold there, brought on even more sectional troubles, and while Henry Clay's compromise proposal in 1850 averted a showdown, the debate over slavery in the Kansas and Nebraska territories provoked anger all over again. The delicate balance that men of reason had striven so long and so hard to achieve was now ruined.

Deeply disturbed by this grave turn of affairs, which caused bloody local battles on the Missouri-Kansas border, Oliver Wendell Holmes produced his humorous metaphorical poem "The Deacon's Masterpiece, or the Wonderful 'One-Hoss Shay'." Holmes narrated a tale of a seemingly indestructible carriage built by a parson in 1775:

Now in building of chaises, I tell you what,
There is always somewhere *a weakest spot—*
In hub, tire, felloe, in spring or thill,
In panel, or crossbar, or floor, or sill,
In screw, bolt, thoroughbrace—lurking still,
Find it somewhere you must and will—

But the Deacon's shay appears to be permanently durable—until precisely one hundred years after its construction:

Eighteen Hundred—it came and found
The Deacon's Masterpiece strong and sound.
Eighteen hundred increased by ten—
"Hahnsum kerridge" they called it then.
Eighteen hundred and twenty came—
Running as usual; much the same.
Thirty and forty at last arrive,
And then come fifty, and fifty-five.

On the first of November, 1855, there are "traces of age in the one-hoss shay."

The parson was working his Sunday's text—
Had got to fifthly, *and stopped perplexed*
At what the—Moses—was coming next.
All at once the horse stood still,
Close by the meet'n'-house on the hill.
First a shiver, and then a thrill,
Then something decidedly like a spill. . . .
What do you think the parson found,
When he got up and stared around?
The poor old chaise in a heap or mound,
As if it had been to the mill and ground!

The end of the "one-hoss shay."

You see, of course, if you're not a dunce,
How it went to pieces all at once—
All at once and nothing first—
Just as bubbles do when they burst. . . .

While the poem could be read as merely a piece of whimsy, it was taken for an allegory of the Union: the American government was falling apart, the weakness being not in any single part but in its essence. Collapse did not follow in 1855, but by the end of the decade nothing could prevent the dissolution of the Republic. The election of Abraham Lincoln sounded the trumpet for secession of the Southern states; before cooler heads could prevail, bombs were bursting in midair over Fort Sumter.

Almost all of the humorists known nationally rallied to the Northern cause, and Lincoln could boast a "kitchen cabinet" of magnificent wits to keep his spirits up and advise him on popular reactions to his measures. Lincoln, it is well known, loved a good joke, and though he drew severe criticism for reciting funny anecdotes in front of congressmen or foreign ministers even in times of dire menace—one wit suggested that Lincoln was in his "anecdotage"—he excused his levity with the explanation that "With the fearful strain of war upon me, if I did not laugh I should die."

One of the President's favorite comics was Artemus Ward, whom Lincoln quoted so often people started calling him the Court Jester. Ward's creator was Charles Farrar Brown, a New Englander who had sought his newspaper fortunes in Ohio. Brown gave Ward the character of an itinerant showman who exhibits wax figures and a menagerie of peculiar animals, and the scrappy pluck of Artemus is a quality that would certainly endear him to the Chief of State. In one episode, Ward relates how, during a tour of his show through the South, a mob of Alabamians demand that he haul down the Stars and Stripes:

> "We air cum, Sir," said a millingtary man in a cockt hat, "upon a hi and holy mishun. The Southern Eagle is screamin threwout this sunny land—proudly and defiantly screamin, Sir!"
>
> "What's the matter with him," sez I, "don't his vittles sit well on his stummick?"
>
> "That Eagle, Sir, will continner to scream all over this brite and tremenjus land!"
>
> "Wall, let him *scream*. If your eagle can amuse hisself by screamin, let him went!" . . .

For refusing to take down the flag, Ward is arrested and his show confiscated. After being "carrid to Montgomry in iuns and placed in durans vial," Ward gets to see Jefferson Davis, President of the Confederacy. And here, though the language is comic, Ward draws a crucial distinction to explain the position held by most Northerners—including Lincoln himself:

> Many of us was your sincere frends, and thought certain parties amung us was fussin about you and meddling with your consarns intirely too much. But J. Davis, the minit you fire a gun at the piece of dry-goods called the Star Spangled Banner, the North gits up and rises en massy, in defense of that banner. Not agin you as individooals—not agin the South even—but to save the flag. . . . So we shall hate to whip the naughty South, but we must do it if you don't make back tracks at onct, and we shall wallup you out of your boots! J. Davis, it is my decided opinion that the Sonny South is makin a egrejus mutton-hed of herself!

Another great humorist was David Ross Locke, a New Yorker who, like the creator of Artemus Ward, settled in Ohio to take up the newspaper trade. In 1860 Locke, in his *Bucyrus Journal,* introduced the character of Petroleum V. Nasby, a swindler, a bully, a drunkard, an opportunist, and all in all a pretty unsavory individual. Locke was a more indignant man than his friend Charles Farrar Brown, and accordingly drew the character of Nasby much more unpleasantly than Brown had drawn that of Artemus Ward. But in depicting Nasby as a scoundrel, Locke could hold up the vices of his time to his countrymen and shame them.

One of the biggest problems for the President then, as it is today, was the draft. Most soldiers who fought early in the war were volunteers, but after the first flush of enthusiasm passed it became harder and harder to get men to enlist. Lincoln was forced to institute a draft. The excuses his draft boards heard were hilarious, and some of Petroleum V. Nasby's were fairly representative:

> I see in the papers last nite, that the Goverment hez institooted a draft, and that in a few weeks sum hunderds uv thousands uv peesable citizens will be dragged to the tented feeld. I know not wat uthers may do, but ez fer me, I can't go. Upon a rigid eggsaminashen uv my fizzlekle man, I find it wood be wus ner madnis fer me 2 undertake a campane, to-wit:
>
> 1. I'm bald-headid, and hev bin obliged to ware a wig these 22 yeres.
> 2. I heve dandruff in wat scanty hair still hangs around my venerable temples.
> 3. I heve a chronic katarr.
> 4. I hev lost, sence Stanton's order to draft, the use uv wun eye entirely, and hev chronic inflammashen in the other.
> 5. My teeth is all unsound, my palit aint eggsactly rite, and I hev hed bronkeetis 31 yeres last Joon. At present I hev a koff, the paroxisms uv wich is friteful 2 behold.
> 6. I'm holler-chestid, am short-winded, and hev alluz hed panes in my back and side. . . .

A third comic who kept the North laughing was Robert Henry Newell, writing under the name Orpheus C. Kerr. Kerr's main concern was the prosecution of the military operation itself, an enterprise which tried Lincoln desperately. Kerr attacked every aspect of the war effort—the cowardice of generals, the laxness of troop discipline, the corruption of munitions-makers, and the confusion of bureaucrats; and, unlike many of his colleagues, he didn't hesitate to turn on Lincoln himself when the situation warranted it.

Kerr also departed from the convention of regional dialect, couching his satires in straightforward English. The following passage is taken from a letter of his entitled "The Latest Improvements in Artillery":

> By invitation of a well-known official, I visited the Navy-Yard yesterday, and witnessed the trial of some newly-invented rifled cannon. The trial was of short duration, and the jury brought in a verdict of "innocent of any intent to kill."
>
> The first gun was similar to those used in the Revolution, except that it had a larger touch-hole, and the carriage was painted green, instead of blue. This novel and ingenious weapon was pointed at a target about sixty yards distant. It didn't hit it, and as nobody saw any ball, there was much perplexity expressed. A midshipman did say that he thought the ball must have run out of the touch-hole when they loaded up—for which he was instantly expelled from the service. After a long search without finding the ball, there was some thought of summoning the Naval Retiring Board to decide on the matter, when somebody happened to look into the mouth of the cannon, and discovered that the ball hadn't gone out at all. The inventor said this would happen sometimes, especially if you didn't put a brick over the touch-hole when you fired the gun. The government was so pleased with this explanation, that it ordered forty of the guns on the spot, at two hundred thousand dollars apiece. The guns to be furnished as soon as the war is over. . . .

The author of this selection, Orpheus C. Kerr, named himself for one of Lincoln's most discouraging miseries, the office-seeker. Lincoln was no sooner elected than a veritable avalanche of petitioners buried him with pleas to find them places in his administration. Almost invariably they were without any saving virtue but persistence, and the President found it hard to deny anyone claiming respectable qualifications. "I have one vice," he lamented, "and I can call it nothing else: it is not to be able to say 'No.' Thank God for not making me a woman, but if He had, I suppose He would have made me just as ugly as He did, and no one would have tempted me." The throng of office-seekers provided humorists of the day with endless amusement, not all of it without a tinge of pathos as we realize what a strain their constant pleas must have put on the President. Artemus Ward, describing a fictional interview with Lincoln, portrays the leader as crying out:

> "Good God! . . . they cum upon me from the skize—down the chimneys, and from the bowels of the yearth." He hadn't more'n got them words out of his delikit mouth [Ward narrates] before two fat offiss-seekers from Wisconsin, in endeverin to crawl atween his legs for the purpuss of applyin for the tollgateship at Milwawky, upsot the President eleck, & he would hev gone sprawlin into the fireplace if I hadn't caught him in these arms.

Petroleum V. Nasby could be expected to be among those harassing Lincoln for a job, and here were his qualifications:

> 1st. I want a offis.
> 2d. I need a offis
> 3d. A offis wood suit me; ther4
> 4th. I shood like to hev a offis.
>
> I maik no boasts uv what my speshul clames air, but I hev dun the party sum servis.

No one was more humorous about the impostors and freeloaders who crowded in on him than Lincoln himself. "A fellow once came to me to ask for an appointment as a minister abroad," Lincoln related. "Finding he could not get that, he came down to some more modest position. Finally, he asked to be made a tidewaiter [a customs official of the day]. When he saw he could not get that, he asked me for an old pair of trousers. It is sometimes well to be humble," the President concluded.

Lincoln ranked with the best humorists of the time, a veritable reservoir of stories, proverbs, anecdotes, jokes, and ironies which he employed whenever the appropriate situation demanded it—and sometimes, to the exasperation of his cabinet, whenever an inappropriate situation demanded it as well. Of all his trials, the snail's pace of the war was the worst, yet in no situation did his humor shine brighter. At the outset of the war, for instance, Lincoln is supposed to have expressed his exasperation with the reluctant George B. McClellan, commander of the army, in these terms:

My Dear McClellan:
If you don't want to use the army I should like to borrow it for a while.

Yours respectfully,
A. Lincoln

McClellan's excuses for tardiness in launching an offensive were lack of sufficient manpower, equipment, or troop training to guarantee victory. Lincoln began to suspect that for McClellan no amount would be enough. When someone asked the President to estimate the size of the Confederate army, he answered, "About one million

HONEST

ABE'S JOKES:

A.LINCOLN
LAWYER

ING AUTHENTIC JOKES AND SQUIBS

OF

ABRAHAM LINCOLN.

Lincoln ranked with the best humorists of the time.

two hundred thousand men according to the best authority." When his interrogator expressed surprise at the size of the estimate, Lincoln explained, "You see, all our generals, when they get whipped, say the enemy outnumbered them three or five to one, and I must believe them. We have four hundred thousand men in the field."

Though the war itself had the same terrors and horrors that war had always had, it also had moments of comic relief, and the American knack for story-telling could frequently convert the grim elements of battle into a side-splitting yarn. One of the best of these was "The Private History of a Campaign That Failed." It told of a twenty-five-year-old volunteer in a Missouri company of Confederate soldiers; the boy's name was Sam Clemens —he would later call himself Mark Twain. Twain's narrative had that universal quality that could serve as a prototype for the humorous literature of any war. Take the example of his company's retreat from an enemy whose existence was largely rumor:

> It was after nine when we reached Mason's stile at last; and then before we could open our mouths to give the countersign several dogs came bounding over the fence with great riot and noise, and each of them took a soldier by the slack of his trousers and began to back away with him. We could not shoot the dogs without endangering the persons they were attached to; so we had to look on helpless at what was perhaps the most mortifying spectacle of the Civil War. There was light enough and to spare, for the Masons had now run out on the porch with candles in their hands. The old man and his son came and undid the dogs without difficulty, all but Bowers's; but they couldn't undo his dog, they didn't know his combination; he was of the bull kind and seemed to be set with a Yale time-lock, but they got him loose at last with some scalding water.

But lying very close to the surface of war humor was the gruesome specter of death. In fact, it was the very nearness of death that made the humor so zestful, for few could be sure their laughter would not dissolve instantly into sobs of profoundest despair. In his "Private History of a Campaign That Failed," Twain pauses to bring the reader back to cruel reality with a description of his group's ambush of a solitary rider. It chills us even today, and no antiwar statement written since could be more effective:

> When we got to him the moon revealed him distinctly. He was lying on his back with his arms abroad, his mouth was open and his chest heaving with long gasps, and his white shirtfront was all splashed with blood. The thought shot through me that I was a murderer, that I had killed a man, a man who had never done me any harm. That was the coldest sensation that ever went through my marrow. I was down by him in a moment, helplessly stroking his forehead, and I would have given anything then—my own life freely—to make him again what he had been five minutes before.

The Union was preserved, at a price almost too dreadful to relate, a price which this nation pays to this day. Painfully, the humorists returned to their civilian jobs, but it would be a long time before they could free their funnybones for that easy, natural laughter of the innocent days before the war. A few of them took on permanent shadows of seriousness. David Ross Locke, for example, crusaded indefatigably for constitutional amendments that would capture the idea that so many had sacrificed their lives to defend. Two years after the War, Locke—creator of that rascal Petroleum V. Nasby—lectured solemnly on the position of the Negro in

Petroleum V. Nasby, Mark Twain, and Josh Billings.

America in phrases which might have been written yesterday:

> I would not make them superior to the white. I would do nothing more for them than I would do for other men. But I would not prevent them from doing for themselves. I should tear down all bars to their advancement. I would let them make of themselves all that they may. In a republic there should be no avenue to honor or well-doing closed to any man. If they outstrip me in the race, it proves them to be more worthy, and they are clearly entitled to the advantages resulting. . . . I demand, in our renewed and purified republic, the abrogation of all laws discriminating against them. . . . I demand it, because I believe governments were instituted on earth for the protection of the weak against the strong, and that in a republic the ballot is the weak man's only protection. I demand it, because we cannot afford to give the lie to our professions; because we cannot afford to say to the world one thing and do another.

The sign of a good comedian is that he knows when to be serious. The conclusion of the Civil War was such a time. Through the orgy of bloodletting, boys had become men, and the young nation had become a young adult. The innocent dream of our forefathers had exploded into a nightmare of reality, and though much humor was to come, half a century would pass before Americans recovered anything of that wide-eyed ingenuousness that made for the first great age of American wit.

Part II:

The Laughter of Maturity

7

Prince of Jesters

ALTHOUGH MOST OF THE BEST HUMOR OF THE POSTWAR period was published in Western newspapers, the world of American letters stopped far short of taking any Western humorists seriously. No matter what their accomplishments, they were still thought of as clowns. Even the greatest of them was scarcely recognized as much more than the greatest of clowns. It tells much about America to understand why.

The main reason was that Eastern literary snobbery still reigned tenaciously over our cultural thought. In such cities as Boston, New York, Philadelphia, and Baltimore the book-publishing trade was located, and with few exceptions the editorial and critical world of nineteenth-century America was controlled by Easterners. The Brahmins still reigned over taste; it must be remembered that many of the Cambridge group—Emerson, Longfellow, Holmes, Lowell, Whittier—lived long beyond the Civil War into the 1880's and 1890's.

These Easterners, living as they did on the shores of the Atlantic, still thought in Anglo-American terms. They found it difficult to separate the American cultural tradition from the English. Though they called loudly and eloquently for a native form of writing, they could never quite rid themselves of their dependency on Continental criteria. There was, they felt, something not quite worthy about a Western writer, one undisciplined by Eastern schooling or refined by the religious and cultural heritage of New England. And so, while hailing publicly the advent of Westerners, they frowned in private, as if coonskin-clothed deerslayers had just tracked mud across the floors of their tidy cottages.

The failure of the Brahmins after the Civil War lay in their refusal to embrace the potential of the West. At best they could step up and shake its hand politely. But whatever their attitude, the West continued to blossom, and the most exquisite flower it produced was the wit of Mark Twain.

It was a prairie wildflower, not a bloom produced in an Eastern greenhouse. The earth in which it grew had been irrigated not by the brine of the Atlantic, but rather by the rich, silty water of the Mississippi. Samuel Langhorne Clemens was born in the Great Valley of the River, and if any sea affected his consciousness it was the Pacific; he lived near the place where the Mississippi was joined by the Missouri, a river fed by springs reaching deep into the Rocky Mountains.

Sam Clemens, following the conventional pattern for writers of his day, did apprentice work for a printer, then travelled the length and breadth of the land. By the time he was twenty-two, he had seen more of America than many men see in a lifetime, and the experience had filled his imagination with enough impressions to carry him through the next fifty-three years. In 1857 he returned to his beloved river to learn the art of piloting the boats that plied it. The war, of course, interrupted his career and, as we have seen, opened his eyes to the violence and iniquity of what he was much later to call "the damned human race." Afterwards he plunged into the crucible of the Far West.

There he wrote for the newspapers and came under the influence of wits like Bret Harte and Artemus Ward, and by 1867 he had produced his first important works. Not all of them are available to us, for they were spoken, not written. These were his lectures, the endlessly creative outpouring of America's first major stand-up comic, and perhaps the greatest of them all. For the next forty years he would revisit the towns and cities he had covered as a journeyman, holding up to the light of his judgment the manners of a nation, to the breathless mirth of audiences that paid him fortunes to hear him perform.

Because the generation of which Twain was spokesman thought of itself in relation to the River, the question of dependency on Europe was a remote one. The new American was not only unafraid of what Europeans thought—he was indifferent to it. Having survived a nearly suicidal war, he realized that what we had most to fear was our own self-destructive impulses. But until the entire nation understood this, there would not be an easy dialogue between its Eastern and Western halves.

The breakdown of communications between these two

sections is illustrated by this passage from Twain's *Roughing It*, describing a Westerner's attempt to get a friend buried properly:

> After Buck Fanshaw's inquest, a meeting of the shorthaired brotherhood was held, for nothing can be done on the Pacific coast without a public meeting and an expression of sentiment. Regretful resolutions were passed and various committees appointed; among others, a committee of one was deputed to call on the minister, a fragile, gentle, spiritual new fledgling from an Eastern theological seminary, and as yet unacquainted with the ways of the mines. The committeeman, "Scotty" Briggs, made his visit; and in after days it was worth something to hear the minister tell about it. Scotty was a stalwart rough, whose customary suit, when on weighty official business, like committee work, was a fire helmet, flaming red flannel shirt, patent leather belt with spanner and revolver attached, coat hung over arm, and pants stuffed into boot tops. He formed something of a contrast to the pale theological student. . . .
>
> Being admitted to the presence he sat down before the clergyman, placed his firehat on an unfinished manuscript sermon under the minister's nose, took from it a red silk handkerchief, wiped his brow and heaved a sigh of dismal impressiveness, explanatory of his business. He choked, and even shed tears; but with an effort he mastered his voice and said in lugubrious tones:
>
> "Are you the duck that runs the gospel-mill next door?"
>
> "Am I the—pardon me, I believe I do not understand?"
>
> With another sigh and a half-sob, Scotty rejoined: "Why, you see, we are in a bit of trouble, and the boys thought maybe you would give us a lift, if we'd tackle you—that is, if I've got the rights of it and you are the head of the doxology-works next door."
>
> "I am the shepherd in charge of the flock whose fold is next door."

"The which?"

"The spiritual adviser of the little company of believers whose sanctuary adjoins these premises."

Scotty scratched his head, reflected a moment, and then said: "You ruther hold over me, pard. I reckon I can't call that hand. Ante and pass the buck."

"I beg your pardon. What did I understand you to say?"

"Well, you've ruther got the bulge on me. Or maybe we've both got the bulge, somehow. You don't smoke me and I don't smoke you. You see, one of the boys has passed in his checks, and we want to give him a good sendoff, and so the thing I'm on now is to roust out somebody to jerk a little chin-music for us and waltz him through handsome."

"My friend, I seem to grow more and more bewildered. Your observations are wholly incomprehensible to me. Cannot you simplify them in some way? At first I thought perhaps I understood you, but I grope now. Would it not expedite matters if you restricted yourself to categorical statements of fact unencumbered with obstructing accumulations of metaphor and allegory?"

Another pause, and more reflection. Then, said Scotty: "I'll have to pass, I judge."

"How?"

"You've raised me out, pard."

"I still fail to catch your meaning."

"Why, that last lead of yourn is too many for me—that's the idea. I can't neither trump nor follow suit."

Twain's feud was not so much with the East as with snobbery in general—a trait we have seen running through the American grain from the beginning. It appeared to be with the East only because so much American snobbery seemed to originate there. Singled out for special attention were those civilized individuals who pretended to extensive experience in wild nature, but who had never really ventured much farther than the woods at the edge of town. Once and for all, Twain was going to show the world that a man didn't have to sport London haberdashery and a Harvard accent to be regarded as a civilized gentleman; on the contrary, such furnishings were often the mark of a fool, a knave, or a hypocrite.

As evidence, Twain chose to hold up to ridicule the work of James Fenimore Cooper, whose "authentic" tales of woodsmen and savages were as much the international rage then as Ian Fleming's spy thrillers were to be a century later. To Twain they represented as much real understanding of backwoods nature and savagery as might be possessed by a Parisian courtier, and in his attack on "Fenimore Cooper's Literary Offenses" he poured out his contempt for the fraud perpetrated by this presumptuous Brahmin. Here is just one delicious excerpt:

> The ark is arriving at the stream's exit now, whose width has been reduced to less than twenty feet to accommodate the Indians—say to eighteen. There is a foot to spare on each side of the boat. Did the Indians notice that there was going to be a tight squeeze there? Did they notice that they could make money by climbing down out of that arched sapling and just stepping aboard when the ark scraped by? No, other Indians would have noticed these things but Cooper's Indians never notice anything. . . .
>
> The ark is one hundred and forty feet long; the dwelling is ninety feet long. The idea of the Indians is to drop softly and secretly from the arched sapling to the dwelling as the ark creeps along under it at the rate of a mile an hour, and butcher the family. It will take the ark a minute and a half to pass under. It will take the ninety-foot dwelling a minute

to pass under. Now, then, what did the six Indians do? . . . Their chief, a person of quite extraordinary intellect for a Cooper Indian, warily watched the canal-boat as it squeezed along under him and when he had got his calculations fined down to exactly the right shade, as he judged, he let go and dropped. And *missed the house!* . . .

There still remained in the roost five Indians. The boat has passed under and is now out of their reach. Let me explain what the five did—you would not be able to reason it out for yourself. No. 1 jumped for the boat but fell in the water astern of it. Then No. 2 jumped for the boat but fell in the water still farther astern of it. Then No. 3 jumped for the boat and fell a good way astern of it. Then No. 4 jumped for the boat and fell in the water *away* astern. Then even No. 5 made a jump for the boat—for he was a Cooper Indian. In the matter of intellect, the difference between a Cooper Indian and the Indian that stands in front of the cigar shop is not spacious.

Twain's contentions with snobbery and pomposity were soon to extend beyond the Atlantic seaboard. In 1867 he arranged to go on a grand tour of Europe and the Mediterranean countries along with a number of "select" travellers. The result of that voyage was *Innocents Abroad*, a masterpiece which can be said to have established our native humor like a flag planted victoriously on an enemy hill. There is scarcely a page in it that doesn't sparkle with Twain's charming wonder, admiration, and enthusiasm, as if he really were an innocent whose eyes were being opened for the first time by the splendor across the sea.

But Mark Twain was not innocent. Between the lines of his awe is a hearty sarcasm. However high his flights of appreciation, he never really loses a certain detachment.

It is this standoffish attitude that truly differentiates him from all the other Americans who went to Europe before him. Franklin, Irving, Emerson—they had all been on shaky ground in Europe because they lacked confidence in the strength of their homeland. Their pride in America had always been tempered by embarrassment, like that of parents who say to strangers, "My child is actually very lively, but not in front of company."

But Mark Twain made no apologies for his nation. On the contrary, he was always ready to put up a stiff fight to defend America's ways. He was willing to concede Europe its superiorities, but he was not about to give away points it didn't merit. If some of his companions were carried away by their foreign experience, Mark Twain remained the dispassionate Yankee observer. He could no more conceive of being "converted" by the Old World than he could of changing his nationality.

And there is the heart of the matter: he, and America, had a distinct nationality now. Else how could an American travel to Europe and dare find it—amusing?

It was amusing because Twain, who had seen so much of human vice, folly, and wickedness, could not be taken in by them even when disguised under foreign languages, manners, and polish. A rogue was a rogue, whether he called himself a card sharp, a James Fenimore Cooper, or the King of France. In fact, once he got his bearings abroad Twain could not only spot chicanery but give back as good as he got, as witness this episode in which he and a friend "put on" a French waiter:

> We ferreted out another French imposition—a frequent sign to this effect: "ALL MANNER OF AMERICAN DRINKS ARTISTICALLY PREPARED HERE." We

procured the services of a gentleman experienced in the nomenclature of the American bar, and moved upon the works of one of these impostors. A bowing, aproned Frenchman skipped forward and said: *"Que voulez les messieurs?"* I do not know what *Que voulez les messieurs* means but such was his remark.

Our general said "We will take a whisky-straight."

(A stare from the Frenchman.)

"Well, then, give us a sherry cobbler."

(A stare and a shrug.)

The Frenchman was checkmated. This was all Greek to him.

"Give us a brandy smash!"

The Frenchman began to back away, suspicious of the ominous vigor of the last order—began to back away, shrugging his shoulders and spreading his hands apologetically.

The General followed him up and gained a complete victory. The uneducated foreigner could not even furnish a Santa Cruz Punch, an Eye-Opener, a Stone-Fence or an Earthquake. It was plain that he was a wicked impostor.

Elsewhere in the book, Twain and his friends have some fun at the expense of an Italian guide:

He has marched us through miles of pictures and sculpture in the vast corridors of the Vatican; and enough miles of picture and sculpture in twenty other palaces; he has shown us the great picture in the Sistine Chapel, and frescoes enough to fresco the heavens—pretty much all done by Michael Angelo. So with him we have played the game that has vanquished so many guides for us—imbecility and idiotic questions. These creatures never suspect—they have no idea of a sarcasm.

He shows us a figure and says: "Statoo brunzo." (Bronze statue)

"We look at it indifferently and the doctor asks: "By Michael Angelo?"

"No—not know who."

Then he shows us the ancient Roman Forum. The doctor asks "Michael Angelo?"

A stare from the guide. "No—a thousan' year before he is born."

Then an Egyptian obelisk. Again: "Michael Angelo?"

"Oh, *mon dieu,* genteelmen! Zis is *two* thousan' year before he is born!"

He grows so tired of that unceasing question sometimes, that he dreads to show us anything at all. The wretch has tried all the ways he can think of to make us comprehend that Michael Angelo is only responsible for the creation of a *part* of the world, but somehow he has not succeeded yet. Relief for overtasked eyes and brain from study and sight-seeing is necessary, or we shall become idiotic sure enough. Therefore the guide must continue to suffer. If he does not enjoy it, so much the worse for him. We do.

In the light of all of Twain's teasing of Europeans, the title of his book *Innocents Abroad* takes on a vivid double meaning. Who were the real innocents abroad, the Americans or the Europeans? Ben Franklin's literary hoaxes on the Europeans had uncovered a blind spot in them: a stolid certainty of their superiority. That blind spot made them as vulnerable in their way as Americans were in *theirs*, and the way Mark Twain exploited it was his way of declaring that henceforth America would be nobody's fool. There were innocents abroad, all right—but they were there before the Americans arrived.

He was to bring his teasing to the level of art in his *A Connecticut Yankee in King Arthur's Court.* This book is an allegory of the honest Yankee grappling with the

Hank as "Sir Boss," the hero of A Connecticut Yankee.

corruption and hypocrisy of the Old World, a world represented by the inane superstition of Merlin the Magician. Hank, the hero who has somehow been transported to the court from Connecticut of the 1880's, is perpetually struggling with Merlin to bring enlightenment, justice, reason, and democratic fairness to the benighted people of the Middle Ages. But, like the Europeans of Twain's time, they are too deeply mired in their complacency to accomplish anything important for themselves. A memorable example of this can be seen in this contest between Hank and Merlin:

> We had a solemn stage-wait now for about twenty minutes, a thing I had counted on for effect; it is always good to let your audience have a chance to work up its expectancy. At length, out of the silence a noble Latin chant—men's voices—broke and swelled up and rolled away into the night, a majestic tide of melody. I had put that up too, and it was one of the best effects I ever invented. When it was finished I stood up on the platform and extended my hands abroad for two minutes, with my face uplifted—that always produces a dead hush—and then slowly pronounced this ghastly word with a kind of awfulness which caused hundreds to tremble, and many women to faint:
>
> **"Constantinopolitanischerdudelsackspfeifenmachersgesellschafft!"**
>
> Just as I was moaning out the closing hunks of that word I touched off one of my electric connections, and all that murky world of people stood revealed in a hideous blue glare! It was immense—that effect! Lots of people shrieked, women curled up and quit in every direction, foundlings collapsed by platoons. The abbot and the monks crossed themselves nimbly and their lips fluttered with agitated prayers. Merlin held his grip but he was astonished clear down to his corns; he had never seen anything to begin with that before.

Twain believed that the Old World's attempt to resist democratic attitudes was literally something out of the Dark Ages, and it is no accident that he chose King Arthur's Court to set his book in. But while Europe's blindness to the new wave of thought coming from America was often merely amusing to Twain, he was aware of a deeper, darker, and truly wicked aspect of that blindness. Another passage from *A Connecticut Yankee* demonstrates this:

> We were off before sunrise, Sandy riding and I limping along behind. In half an hour we came upon a group of ragged poor creatures who had assembled to mend the thing which was regarded as a road. They were as humble as animals to me, and when I proposed to breakfast with them, they were so flattered, so overwhelmed by this extraordinary condescension of mine that at first they were not able to believe that I was in earnest. My lady put up her scornful lip and withdrew to one side; she said in their hearing that she would as soon think of eating with the other cattle—a remark which embarrassed these poor devils merely because it referred to them and not because it insulted or offended them, for it didn't. And yet they were not slaves, not chattels. By a sarcasm of law and phrase they were freemen. Seven-tenths of the free population of the country were of just their class and degree: small "independent" farmers, artisans, etc., which is to say they were the nation, the actual Nation; they were about all of it that was useful or worth saving or really respectworthy, and to subtract them would have been to subtract the Nation and leave behind some dregs, some refuse, in the shape of a king, nobility, and gentry, idle, unproductive, acquainted mainly with the arts of wasting and destroying and of no sort of use or value in any rationally constructed world.

Twain was by no means insensitive to the shortcomings of democracy; it is just that he had been more able to tolerate them in his youth. As he grew older a change began to come over him. The exuberance he had felt for life turned sour. A series of private griefs weakened his laugh-muscles, and the scandalous corruption of the postwar era reached such proportions that he was faced with either joining the head-over-heels chase for money, or lapsing into cynicism. He took the latter course. His book *The Gilded Age*, describing life in this era, reflects the growing darkness of his view of life. His declining faith in the goodness of democracy and the nobility of the common man can be seen in the closing words of a sermon, delivered by a Senator up for re-election:

> "My precious children, love your parents, love your teachers, love your Sunday-school, be pious, be obedient, be honest, be diligent, and then you will succeed in life and be honored of all men. Above all things, my children, be honest. Above all things be pure-minded as the snow. Let us join in prayer."
>
> When Senator Dilworthy departed from Cattleville, he left three dozen boys behind him arranging for a campaign of life whose objective point was the United States Senate.
>
> When he arrived at the state capital at midnight Mr. Noble came and held a three hours' conference with him, and then as he was about leaving said: "I've worked hard, and I've got them at last. Six of them haven't got quite backbone enough to slew around and come right out for you on the first ballot tomorrow, but they're going to vote against you on the first for the sake of appearances, and then come out for you all in a body on the second—I've fixed all that! By supper-time tomorrow you'll be re-elected. You can go to bed and sleep easy on that."
>
> After Mr. Noble was gone, the Senator said: "Well, to bring about a complexion of things like this was worth coming West for."

Twain's good nature declined even more sharply in the last years of his life, and the productions of that period are scant of any but the blackest humor. Yet, as we shall see, the times themselves were black, and it would take younger, fresher, more vigorous wits than the aging Twain to find anything to laugh about in the last quarter of the nineteenth century in America. Those wits would look to him, however, for their inspiration, and would remember not his bitterness but the sunny flashes of faith he could still manage to radiate in those latter years. A letter to Andrew Lang written in 1890 reaffirms his belief in the common people, the future strength of America:

> The thin crust of humanity—the cultivated—are worth pacifying, worth pleasing, worth coddling, worth nourishing and preserving with dainties and delicacies, it is true: but to be caterer to that little faction is no very dignified occupation, it seems to me; it is merely feeding the over-fed, and there must be small satisfaction in that. It is not that little minority who are already saved that are best worth lifting at, I should think, but the mighty mass of uncultivated people who are underneath. . . . I have never tried in even one single little instance to help cultivate the cultivated classes. I was not equipped for it, either by native gifts or training. And I never had any ambition in that direction, but always hunted for bigger game—the masses.

Twain never realized just how big was the game he bagged. For not only did he thrill and delight the masses of his own day—what is called the "horizontal" audience—but those of the next day as well, the "vertical" one. Not only do we still read him with fresh glee, but many of us were privileged to see him revived by a brilliant impersonator, Hal Holbrook. Holbrook captured every nuance of dress, voice, and delivery in his stage and television *tour de force*, *Mark Twain Tonight*, allowing us an unforgettable evening with the prince of jesters.

8

The Age of Frowns

IT WOULD BE AN OVERSIMPLIFICATION TO SAY THAT THE thirty-five years between the end of the Civil War and the turn of the century were humorless. There were many men of wit, much laughter, and much to laugh about. But if we compare this period to the one in which the Western writers had flourished, it becomes obvious that a certain gusto had gone out of American life, with nothing to replace it. The character of the American people at this time appears to have been a solemn one. And just as it is interesting to read about why people laughed in one age, it can be interesting to learn why they did not in another.

In the first place, the impact of the Civil War decimated the male population: 617,000 men, most of them in the bloom of manhood, had died in the four-year carnage;

375,000 more had been injured; countless more had been so badly affected by imprisonment or the mere shock of warfare that their return to civilian life was more of a burden on the nation than an infusion of vitality into the bloodstream of the Reconstruction era.

It has been argued, with some validity, that many men who survived the war were cowards, draft-dodgers, deserters, and scoundrels. The most honorable, courageous, and selfless men had enlisted at the outset of the war to fight for their convictions, and it was invariably they who rushed their enemy's breastworks and stormed their trenches to fall before withering volleys—while their less gallant companions trampled over their bodies to finish the campaign. It is not an altogether accurate view, but there can be no doubt that while plenty of men existed at the war's end to exploit possibilities of corruption and knavery, not enough existed to resist such depredations. We have to consider, too, that even the honest, hearty lads who did survive the war with body and soul intact carried, to the end of their lives, memories of horror and sorrow that could not be dislodged by any amount of humor. And we must remember that many private citizens who lived on to 1900—families of dead and maimed soldiers, planters whose farms had been plundered and burned, and others ruined by the war—had had the spirit of laughter ground out of their systems.

North or South, town or city, the postwar nation was in depressing condition. The South was a shambles, and its attempts to pick itself up were constantly crippled by the ruthless pillaging of its resources by carpetbaggers and other unscrupulous men. The Eastern seaboard, fortress of American civilization, after suffering major

Those who survived the Civil War had had the spirit of laughter ground out of their systems.

losses in the war, continued to be drained by the westward migration of its population as hordes headed for gold- and land-rushes. New Hampshire, for instance, shrank in population from 326,073 in 1850 to 318,300 in 1870. Farmers deserted the rocky New England soil for the fabled black earth of the Midwest, and one historian guessed that "more than a million acres cultivated in

1850 had gone back to pasture and woodland in 1900." On the other hand, eastern cities swelled with the influx of immigrants from Europe. The conditions in which they lived were far from conducive to laughter, but even if they did manage to wring some laughter out of their suffering, they joked in alien tongues, and the humor was lost on us.

The cities swelled because the Industrial Revolution, reaching boom proportions in the late nineteenth century, demanded workers in urban factories. As these workers became trapped in the cycle of inadequate wages and the high cost of living, their dream of prosperity and freedom—the very same dream that had transported the pilgrims to our shores two hundred and fifty years earlier—withered. In place of that dream was the reality of squalid neighborhoods, sickness and starvation, back-breaking labor and hopeless futures, while cynical industrial, commercial, and financial manipulators—the so-called robber barons—waxed wealthy on their miseries. America had fought a war to free slaves, only to have this new form of slavery imposed upon it.

With the Industrial Revolution would soon come the assembly-line, a system which, for all its advantages to the producer, imposed on the worker a sense of identity with the machine. People were interchangeable, easily maintained, easily replaced, and needed only basic fuels to keep them running smoothly. Towards the end of this era a new philosophy, Marxism and its communistic variations, raised hope for the working classes that they would not have to endure these degrading conditions forever, that their day of revolution would come. This philosophy would soon encounter its own bitter disillusionments, especially in the Russian Revolution and the totalitarian state it brought about, but workers of that day could not foresee this development and clung to their dream. Courageous labor leaders dared speak out against the injustices of the industrial system, and as the century closed, this nation saw the first flexing of unionism's muscles. But the feud between labor and management was one of unimaginable rancor. Whether you were a worker or a capitalist, the issue was money and what it could buy—it was a singularly unfunny subject to most people then.

Was the age utterly devoid of saving values? No, but those we owned were not the kind that made for much mirth. In response to a laxness of frontier morality, an increase of propriety asserted itself among the people of high social standing who set the pace for the rest of society. The looseness of conduct associated with the war and its aftermath was rejected in favor of prudishness and high formality among the rich, the newly rich, and all that aspired to wealth and respectability. Though, as we have seen, the word Puritanism did an injustice to our pilgrim ancestors, it was aptly applied to the character of late nineteenth-century life here. It had its counterpart in the Victorianism of England. With the renewal of interest in England during the Gaslight Age, imitation of British behavior was inevitable. A new aristocracy was emerging in America, based on wealth, and it is not surprising that the morality of the English aristocracy became a model for us. In any case, Victorian-Puritan morality was scarcely a laughing matter.

The Industrial Revolution gave added thrust to the growth of science, leading Henry Adams, direct descendant of two Presidents, to conclude that the worship of science might well replace conventional religion in the twentieth century. He suggested that the dynamo, as a symbol of electrical force, could eventually substitute for the spiritual force represented by the soaring cathedrals of Europe. In another area of science, the conclusions Charles Darwin reached in his *Origin of Species* were sending the Age of Reason onto a collision course with the Age of Faith, a collision which had been a long time coming. Demonstrating, by force of thorough research, observation, and experimentation, that the principle underlying biological nature was the natural selection of the fittest members of each species, Darwin by implication was contradicting the biblical dogma that the species as we know them had been created by God. Man had not been placed on earth in one day by miraculous means, but rather had evolved over countless eons from some lower order. In another age, Darwin might have been sent to the stake as a heretic, but because conditions were right, his views were widely accepted in the intellectual community. The result, as these views filtered down to the masses, was a terrible uneasiness as they realized that an old order was threatened. Here again one could find little to be amused over.

But something else had happened to erase the grin from the American face, something often underestimated, but of incalculable significance. It happened at noon of April 22, 1889. At that moment a vast tract of land in the Oklahoma territory was declared open to settlement by homesteaders, by proclamation of President Benjamin Harrison. A shot rang out, and thousands of settlers —on foot, mounted on horseback, in wagons, buckboards, and even stagecoaches, surged forward in a stupendous clamor and cloud of dust. By dusk the territory was not only occupied, but sizable tent cities were erected, cities that became Guthrie and Oklahoma City.

The importance of this event is that this territory had been the last important piece of land in the Continental United States unsettled by Americans. Of course there was and still is much uninhabited land in the United States, but the Oklahoma territory was the last piece in the jigsaw of American territorial expansion. All our land was now accounted for. To put it briefly, the frontier no longer existed.

Four years later, before a group of historians at the Columbian Exposition in Chicago, an American historian named Frederick Jackson Turner read a paper he had written. It expressed an interpretation of American history that had been discussed around the time but never stated in an organized fashion. It stressed his conviction that although the struggle for liberty, the growth of national pride, the democratic spirit, and the slavery issue were important factors in the growth of our national character, it was the existence of a frontier that contributed most powerfully. The Western wilderness, the prairies, the mighty rivers and their valleys, had stimulated Americans to develop those unique traits that we lump under the single quality of individualism. The fresh opportunity that Western land offered shaped the American personality as nothing else had done.

But now, as Turner read his thesis, that frontier was no more. Americans had pushed to the borders of their country—to the Great Lakes and the parallel 54° 40′ on the north, to the Gulf of Mexico and the Rio Grande River on the south, and beyond the Rocky Mountains to the Pacific on the west. Suddenly the escape hatch was shut. The rollicking carefreeness of earlier days was no more; a man could no longer pick up his gear and move on, confident of staking a claim in virgin territory.

Americans were now confronted with the responsibility of developing what they had, of making the most of the inner and outer resources at their disposal. The American dream was challenged as never before; if we did not find new ways of expressing it, it would dry up and shatter. We could not look to land as the source of our most cherished values. The question now was what we did with our land, and what we did on it. This was serious business.

How did our literature reflect the solemnity of the times?

The nature of publishing showed it, for example. Just as the Western humorists had relied on the newspaper as the vehicle for their writing, the postwar men of letters had the magazine. Between 1857—the year of the *Atlantic Monthly*'s founding—and 1885, such magazines as *Harper's Weekly, Century, Galaxy, Overland Monthly, Forum, Appleton's Journal,* and *Lippincott's Magazine* were started. If these names sound ponderous and "literary," that's just what they were. The word "literary" took on the connotation of seriousness, and though Mark Twain, Bret Harte, and other humorists appeared in the pages of these magazines, the burden of their contents was definitely serious. Why?

Newspapers had been appropriate to the Western humorist. They were usually put together in a slapdash way, with deadlines never less than urgent and more often near the panic stage. This suited the spontaneity of the frontier wits, who knocked out their contributions in one sitting, rarely pausing to revise, not caring if some sloppiness got in, because even if they delivered

Some of the magazines published in New York at the end of the nineteenth century.

perfect copy it would probably be cut or published replete with typographical errors. And even if it did get published perfectly, it was questionable whether half the readers would know the difference. What the devil! They weren't writing for posterity anyway.

On the other hand, a magazine was planned months in advance. The formality of its structure required formality of content, and contributors were given guidelines and prohibitions on theme, form, length, and language. Writers, one eye on posterity, had to be more thoughtful about what they said and how they said it, and the long deadlines gave editors a better chance to help writers shape their material until it was close to perfect.

But while this approach was setting the stage for a golden age in American letters, the Western humorists didn't care for it very much. Most of them were what sportswriters call "naturals," their writing being an offshoot of their storytelling talent; yet the forbidding format and high polish required cramped their styles. After asking them to write "sketches," the magazine establishment was asking them to tackle "articles"; after writing "yarns," they were being asked to write "short stories." And the magazines wanted novels to serialize, requiring them to plot carefully, delineate character skillfully, and make the parts consistent with one another. Why, it was as if they were being asked to learn ballroom dancing after a lifetime of nothing but hoedowns.

Thus the fashion in writers swung back to the educated, scholarly man. And while the trend did not swing back to Brahminism, the end of the nineteenth century did belong to a more intellectual type. Another generation would have to pass before we were to see a merging of the rough 'n' ready humorist and the genteel man of letters.

Postwar writers described their literature as Realism or Naturalism. It was concerned with describing life as it really was, rather than in the idealized way seen by Emerson and the New England "transcendental" writers, earlier in the century. It chose immediate topics, not classical ones; it tended to pessimism, dealing with the darker urges of mankind instead of the side closest to the angels. It reflected Darwin's principles, removing much of the wonder with which man had regarded himself until then. In short, the literature of this age was devoted not merely to showing man as he was, but to showing him as possibly worse than anyone had thought he was. Novelists like Henry James, Stephen Crane and Frank Norris attempted to bring fictional mankind closer to the factual mankind uncovered by sociologists, anthropologists, and what we would now call behavioral scientists.

William Dean Howells, editor of the *Atlantic Monthly*, was somewhat disturbed by this trend towards realism, and called on American novelists to turn away from the depressing vein of Russians like Dostoevski, whose work was reaching our shores at the time, and concentrate instead on "the laughing aspects" of life. Humor, Howells felt, was more natural to Americans than its opposite. But the trend had too much momentum to be so easily reversed, and even Howells could not help producing a body of work that hardly captured the "laughing aspects."

There was one group of writers, however, who still took amusement from American life: these were the so-called Local Colorists. They were what might be termed specialists: they concentrated on some small area of the country and delineated it in all its charm and warmth. Such writers as Edward Eggleston of the Middle Border, George Washington Cable and Joel Chandler Harris of the South, and Sarah Orne Jewett of New England, carried on love affairs in print with their own regions. Though none attained the robustness of the old Western bunch, there was still much gaiety in their work. Their ability to make much out of some small detail would foreshadow the humorous essay form that reached a pinnacle in the 1920's and 1930's. Typical is this excerpt from the pen of Charles Dudley Warner, a New Englander:

> I believe that I have found, if not original sin, at least vegetable total depravity in my garden; and it was there before I went into it. It is the bunch, or joint, or snake-grass—whatever it is called. As I do not know the names of all the weeds and plants, I have to do as Adam did in his garden—name things as I find them. This grass has a slender, beautiful stalk: and when you cut it down, or pull up a long root of it, you fancy it is got rid of; but, in a day or two, it will come up in the same spot in half a dozen vigorous blades. . . .
>
> I have said it was total depravity. Here it is. If you attempt to pull up and root out any sin in you, which shows on the surface—if it does not show, you do not care for it—you may have noticed how it runs into an interior network of sins, and an ever-sprouting branch of them roots somewhere; and that you cannot pull one without making a general internal disturbance, and rooting up your whole being. I suppose it is less trouble to quietly cut them off at the top—say once a week on Sunday, when you put on your religious clothes and face—so that no one will see them, and not try to eradicate the network within.

The passage might have been written in the 1930's but for the important fact that by then humorists would have given up drawing morals.

The trouble with the local colorists, of course, is that they were simply—well, local. Though they extolled the uniqueness of their regions, those very regions were being bound together by the stupendous force of industrial development. By the turn of the century the automobile and electricity would spell the end of regional individuality. Anyone who could not see beyond his own vicinity—could not grasp the concept that he was first and above all a citizen of the nation or imagine us taking a role in world politics—would fall behind. The literature of those who fell behind would be called decadent, the product of people living in an isolated past while the rest of the world passed them by. Progress became the byword of the twentieth century, and traditional ways, places, and values would be sacrificed sooner or later to its momentum. It is easy to understand, then, why the local colorists did not laugh too heartily: they were more than a little nervous that their beloved locales would soon be buried by national progress.

But while just about everyone else of his time was either scowling, frowning, smiling timidly, or laughing cynically, one writer was chuckling with genuine gusto. His name was Finley Peter Dunne, and of all the folk philosophers this country has produced, none combined the sharpness of satire with the buffoonery of dialect

Mr. Dooley, created by Finley Peter Dunne, speaks to "Hinnissy."

"Ye're me Circulation. Ye're Small, Hinnissy, but ye're Silict"

better than his character, the Irish barkeeper Mr. Dooley. And only Mr. Dooley stood above the regional, planting his heels from coast to coast to make fun of his age on a *national* basis.

Mr. Dooley's peeve was progress. In his lilting Hibernian accents he would point out again and again that human nature was sadly lagging behind scientific and industrial development, and it might be a good idea to pause in our headlong flight into the twentieth century to decide just what we wanted to do about the problem of *people*.

For example, in the 1890's America, perhaps out of eagerness to continue its thrust towards new frontiers, expanded beyond its natural coastlines. This was thought by some to represent a glorious advance by us into the arena of international power. But others—such as Mr. Dooley—were not that much impressed by our shows of force. They regarded them as the acts of a bully and an imperialist—the very type of behavior we had freed ourselves from in the Revolution. When Admiral Dewey licked the Spanish in Manila Bay in the Philippines in 1898, the triumph was greeted with loud patriotic cheers. But Mr. Dooley was decidedly not overwhelmed by the defeat of a handful of leaky, poorly manned ships. Here is his dialogue with his sidekick Mr. Hennessy:

"I know what I'd do if I was Mack [President McKinley]," said Mr. Hennessy. "I'd hist a flag over th' Ph'lippeens, an' I'd take in th' whole lot iv thim."

"An' yet," said Mr. Dooley, " 'tis not more thin two months since ye larned whether they were islands or canned goods. Ye'er back yard is so small that ye'er cow can't turn r-round without buttin' th' woodshed off th' premises, an' ye wudden't go out to th' stock yards without taken' out a policy on yer life. Suppose ye was standin' at th' corner iv State Sthreet an' Archey R-road, wud ye know what car to take to get to th' Ph'lippeens? If yer son Packy was to ask ye where th' Ph'lippeens is, cud ye give him anny good idea whether they was in Rooshia or jus' west iv th' thracks?"

"Mebbe I cudden't," said Mr. Hennessy, haughtily, "but I'm f'r takin' thim in, annyhow."

"So might I be," said Mr. Dooley, "if I cud on'y get me mind on it. Wan iv the worst things bout this here war is th' way it's makin' puzzles f'r our poor, tired heads. Whin I wint into it, I thought all I'd have to do was to set up here behind th' bar with a good tin-cint see-gar in me teeth, an' toss dinnymite bombs into th' hated city iv Havana. But look at me now. Th' war is still goin' on; an' ivry night, whin I'm countin' up the cash, I'm askin' mesilf will I annex Cubia or lave it to the Cubians? Will I take Porther Ricky [Puerto Rico] or put it by? An' what shud I do with the Ph'lippeens? Oh, what shud I do with thim? I can't annex thim because I don't know where they ar-re. I can't let go iv thim because some wan else'll take thim if I do. . . ."

As the century closed, Americans found themselves standing at a crossroads, asking themselves, with Henry Adams, whether they would become the masters of the empire they had created—or the slaves and victims. One could follow the genial expansiveness of Walt Whitman, or the cross misanthropy of Mark Twain; the nation could go either way, to its glory or to its doom. As the roll of European war drums began to resound in American ears, Americans wondered more and more what role they would be called on to play in the shrinking world. Whatever it was, they would certainly have to summon their sense of humor to see them through.

9

The New Century: Should We Laugh or Cry?

AMERICA'S DIVIDED STATE OF MIND CARRIED OVER INTO THE 1900's and 1910's. It bore some resemblance to attitudes a century earlier, after the Revolution. In both cases the nation had emerged from a war to find itself faced with the responsibility of being united. In both cases it had reacted shyly, uncertain about the way to use its gains. Having achieved its dream, it had no new dream to strive for. By 1900 it was potentially the mightiest industrial, farming, and trading nation the world had ever seen, but that meant taking a role in world affairs. The thought was too much for most Americans, many of whose grandfathers recalled George Washington's warning about getting ensnared in foreign entanglements, and many of whose fathers remembered James Monroe's warning to Europe to stay out of affairs on our side of the Atlantic.

As Emerson had said when asked to join the utopian community of Brook Farm, it was hard enough fighting the battle of his chickencoop without taking on the world. There were monumental internal problems to be licked in this country. If our leaders were uncertain about a foreign policy, it was forgivable. A nation must be strong and harmonious before entering the world arena. And so, except for Teddy Roosevelt's little adventures, America took a stance of isolationism. Affairs in Europe were simmering and would come to a violent boil in 1914, sucking us into involvement whether we desired it or not, but in the first decade of the new century few Americans were eager to be drawn into foreign affairs.

And so we concentrated on our internal affairs. The rise of industrial and financial trusts, which had concentrated almost enough power to match the government's, were at last attacked by a Congress courageous enough to overcome its own vested interest in corruption. Labor unionism, after struggling ferociously with management, began achieving gains that gave the working man a fighting chance to put his hands on some of the prosperity and raise himself above the subsistence level. The farmer, always a victim of natural disasters, uncertain markets, and unscrupulous landholders, found champions in the government to help him escape the cycle of self-defeat. Even women found relief from the age-old denial of their right to vote, achieving suffrage in state after state until it was made federal law.

Were Americans laughing these days? Yes they were, but not in print. Their chief sources of entertainment were vaudeville and movies. The former, brought to perfection by masters like Flo Ziegfeld, was an outgrowth of many traditions including the circus, burlesque, light opera, and the comic monologue perfected by Artemus Ward and Mark Twain. Movies were a crude, flickering version of the modern industry, rarely more at first than filmed vaudeville acts or stage melodramas. But in a society geared to rapid progress, movies were refined into an art form by 1920, and soon Charlie Chaplin was creating his deathless roles in the silents.

Vaudeville and movies had great appeal to the man who, a generation earlier, would have picked up a pen and put it to the task of making people laugh. Many of them had Mark Twain's verbal abilities—though none would ever have them in such abundance—but not the patience or talent to convert those abilities into writing. These men became entertainers. Film especially had a seductive lure for men possessed of the desire to make people laugh. Its visual possibilities beckoned to them like a new frontier, offering them a chance to express the comic spirit in a way never before open to man. This shift to the new medium produced the first generation of film comedy greats.

But alas, it was at the expense of our literature. In the world of the published word, the mood continued solemn. The novel and short story held their supremacy as dominant forms of writing—forms which, we have seen, called for serious intellectual responses from writers. The magazine continued to be the vehicle for those forms. But magazines didn't really reach the majority of Americans. Few had circulations of more than 100,000 in a turn-of-the-century population of 70,000,000. And most books sold far, far fewer than 100,000, or even 10,000, copies. There was still, in other words, plenty of room for printed entertainment. The answer was the newspaper. But the newspaper was in crisis; with the exodus of the great Western comics, a vacuum had been created.

With such large audiences to be tapped, publishers like Joseph Pulitzer and William Randolph Hearst envisioned the money potential of the newspaper. But for that potential to be realized, writers would have to be drawn to the field, writers who could bring a subject to life and convey their excitement to the huge number of literate middle-class people then seeking such stimulation in the vaudeville and nickelodeon shows. Thus newspaper publishers began holding out fists stuffed with money to writers who could endow descriptions of news events with the breathless quality of good fiction.

They found plenty of writers to fill the bill. Many, like Stephen Crane and Jack London, were spoiling for adventure anyway and would probably have written lively copy even if they weren't on a publisher's payroll. They covered disasters and wars for the love of human drama, and their profound involvement in the action and passion of that drama illuminated their reporting with the radiance of bigger-than-life fiction. Newspaper reporting quickly developed into a profession, then an art.

But the restoration of humor to newsprint continued to elude publishers. In attempting to expand circulation, they took up questions of deep concern to common people, slanting their material toward the vivid description of social injustices. Many of the correspondents reporting on them had personally witnessed or been victims of such evils as corporate irresponsibility, stock frauds, child labor, unhealthy food and medical practices, and governmental corruption. They passionately resented the exploitation of decent people and advocated reforms on all fronts.

Therefore, when their causes coincided with the commercial interests of newspaper publishers, a powerful union was the result. It gave rise to the style of journalistic crusade known as muckraking. Publishers like S. S. McClure, Frank A. Munsey and Peter F. Collier engaged the talented services of Lincoln Steffens, Ray Stannard Baker, Ida M. Tarbell, Charles Edward Russell, Edwin Markham, Upton Sinclair, and Samuel Hopkins Adams to expose the many iniquities of the times and to urge legislation against them.

So disgraceful were those iniquities, however, that humor was scarcely appropriate or adequate as a weapon against them. A humorous approach usually suggests that the writer can, if he has to, suffer indignities without fatal damage to body or soul; if things get too bad, he can always move on. But those people suffering indignities early in the twentieth century were far too much oppressed to be able to grin and bear it, and too tightly trapped in the cycle of poverty and injustice to be able to push on.

In the meantime, events in Europe were rapidly militating to draw America away from its excessive concern with itself, and to involve it in the world community. But right up to the moment when Woodrow Wilson declared he could no longer suffer the insults and aggressions of the German nation, Americans remained steadfastly and almost neurotically isolationist. The attitude is delightfully described by Ralph Barton, author of *God's Country*, a comic history of the United States:

While the people of America were wallowing in the output of the national cornucopia, a great war—by far the greatest war that had ever been fought in the history of the universe—broke out in Europe.

So suddenly had the war broken out that the Americans, who had forgotten that Europe existed, found it difficult to realize what had happened. They had simply come down to breakfast one morning and there it was in their newspapers. The big story ran all the way across the top of page one, down the right-hand five columns, and over to page two. As soon as they had ascertained who had won the ball games and fixed the changes of the standings of the teams in their minds, the Americans read of the doings of uhlans and cuirassiers, cossacks and dragoons, hussars and lancers, of fortresses and frontiers, howitzers and shrapnel, of flanking movements and frontal assaults, and the magic words thrilled them to the marrow. They could hear the rattle of musketry as they crushed their corn flakes, and when they dashed their spoons against their teeth they heard sabers clattering against the flagstones of conquered villages. . . .

At last, when the armies had "dug in" and the more spectacular manoeuvres were over, the Americans looked up from their newspapers and began to ask each other—timidly, at first, lest they expose their ignorance—what the war was all about. Presently, when it was discovered that nobody knew, they stopped asking each other, and began telling each other. Small, private wars broke out all over America and the magazines, in the interests of peace, engaged experts to write articles explaining the true causes of the European conflict.

"The war," the articles said, in substance "is the inevitable outcome of deep-seated causes."

That was enough for the majority of the people. They accepted the explanation, adopted it as their own, and announced that they were ready to break anybody's face who disagreed with it.

But with war finally declared, Americans mysteriously reversed direction and flung themselves into the spirit of battle with violent abandon. One reason for this upsurge of enthusiasm was the press, which romanticized the conflict and inspired Americans with the feeling of launching a glorious crusade to save democracy from the Prussian barbarian. A new generation of youth, too young to remember the gruesomeness of the Civil War, pitched in to fight with little anticipation of the gore, mud, death, and despair that awaited them. It was this generation, recoiling in disillusionment after the war, that would call itself "lost."

A few writers like Edward Streeter and Kin Hubbard tried to convey, to their unrealistically patriotic folks back home, something of the realities of life and war overseas, approaching them not as Hemingway was to do but rather in a light vein. Kin Hubbard, for instance, would put them in the form of a letter from a soldier to his mother:

> Well, here I am. I hope you are well. We had some trip comin' over. Cigarettes galore. A piece of shrapnel jest now broke th' last pane o' glass in my window as I write. I have enough terbacker t' last a week. Unless some has been sent since I left I'll probably be without some days before some comes. I'm billeted on th' parlor floor of an ole historic chateau with a mantle piece that goes back t' th' renaissance. My shoes are dryin' on th' mantle. Cigarettes should be mailed at intervals o' two days apart t' assure a steady, unbroken flow. Eatin' t'backer, too, only cigarettes is th' most important. . . . I'm not spendin' any o' my pay as I

want t' loaf a couple o' years when I get home, so any cigarettes or t'backer you send me is jest that much saved. I wouldn' give much fer this historic chateau after th' shrapnel gets thro' with it. . . . You can't carry a pipe over here very handy. Shrapnel knocks 'em out o' your mouth. You bet I've got my three cigarette cases distributed where they'll stop th' most shrapnel. It don't look like I'd ever get my shoes as ther's a constant hail o' shrapnel. Don't worry about me.

Your lovin' son,
STEW.

Despite the almost unbelievable expenditure of life by our French and British allies, Americans seemed to feel they had rescued Europe single-handedly. But instead of remaining abroad to exploit our new-found esteem there, we rode back to our kingdom like some feudal knight, bent on tending our own affairs after performing our good deed. The United States plunged back into isolationism, preferring to mind its own business—and the business of America, as President Coolidge would announce, was business—than to meddle in that of the Old World. Congress refused to ratify President Wilson's commitment to have the United States represented in the League of Nations. Thus, the foremost power on earth forsook its responsibilities and withdrew to leave a power gap that would eventually be filled by the Third Reich.

With the enormous release of energy from wartime tension and austerity, Americans abandoned themselves to financial enterprise with hardly a glance at danger signs of financial instability on the home front or political turbulence on the foreign one. There prevailed a belief that this last war would end all wars, that the future would forever hold peace, prosperity, and mutual good will among nations. There were some pessimists writing, but they were considered crackpots or sore losers grumbling because they weren't sharing in the new prosperity.

The greatest spokesman of these times, ranking among the greatest of any, was H. L. Mencken. Mencken had a profound sense of human dignity, but in the seemingly endless ways in which human beings abused that dignity he found material for three decades of the most pointed satire. His opinions, or "prejudices" as he called them, touched on every subject that affected his countrymen. Few of them did not contribute a genuinely enlightening, as well as entertaining, view. As a student of the American language, he managed to express his sentiments with devastating precision. Though half his readers regarded him as prophet, and the other half as pest, hardly any stood their ground when he levelled his weapons in the direction of their beliefs and behavior. Had Mencken focussed his genius on any single cause he might have been a statesman or captain of industry of historic influence. As it was, his sole ambition was to state the truth about human foolishness, an ambition rarely rewarded generously.

H. L. Mencken's "prejudices" touched every subject that affected his countrymen.

Although Mencken's scorn seemed to know no limits, he was not a bitter man. He maintained his sense of sanity, taking the attitude that if the world wanted to go to the devil it could do so, but that didn't oblige him to give it his blessing. As he said in his preface to the collection he called *A Mencken Chrestomathy*, "My view of the country is predominantly tolerant and amiable. I do not believe in democracy, but I am perfectly willing to admit that it provides the only really amusing form of government ever endured by mankind."

Mencken believed that ever since the early nineteenth century, the masses in America had been wresting the reins of power away from the superior men who traditionally and deservedly ran governments. We have seen this view borne out in the election of Andrew Jackson and the Western influence on the American political system. But now, with the working class making greater and greater strides towards fulfillment, it looked as if the masses would soon be completely in the saddle:

> All government, in its essence, is a conspiracy against the superior man: its one permanent object is to oppress him and cripple him. If it be aristocratic in organization, then it seeks to protect the man who is superior only in law against the man who is superior in fact; if it be democratic, then it seeks to protect the man who is inferior in every way against both. . . . The most dangerous man, to any government, is the man who is able to think things out for himself, without regard to the prevailing superstitions and taboos. . . .
>
> The ideal government of all reflective men, from Aristotle onward, is one which lets the individual alone—one which barely escapes being no government at all. This ideal, I believe, will be realized in the world twenty or thirty centuries after I have passed from these scenes and taken up my public duties in Hell.

The trend of the age, Mencken felt, was to glorify the mediocre, the very worst in mankind:

> Everywhere on earth, save where the enlightment of the modern age is confessedly in eclipse, the movement is toward the completer and more enamored enfranchisement of the lower orders. Down there, one hears, lies a deep, illimitable reservoir of righteousness and wisdom, unpolluted by the corruption of privilege. What baffles statesmen is to be solved by the people, instantly and by a sort of seraphic intuition. Their yearnings are pure; they alone are capable of a perfect patriotism; in them is the only hope of peace and happiness on this lugubrious ball. The cure for the evils of democracy is more democracy.

As a result of the democratic spirit and its fulfillment in the American republic, the superior man must pay tribute to the inferior:

> The mob has its flatterers and bosh-mongers; the king has his courtiers. But there is a difference, and I think it is important. The courtier, at his worst, at least performs his genuflections before one who is theoretically his superior, and is surely not less than his equal. He does not have to abase himself before swine with whom, ordinarily, he would disdain to have any traffic. He is not compelled to pretend that he is a worse man than he really is. He needn't hold his nose in order to approach his benefactor.

And Mencken was keenly aware of the potentially self-destructive quality of democracy. In this passage he puts his finger on a key weakness of our form of government—a weakness which, by the mid-twenties, was beginning to bulge through the fabric of our political and economic system:

> I have spoken hitherto of the possibility that democracy may be a self-limiting disease, like measles. It is, perhaps,

> something more: it is self-devouring. One cannot observe it objectively without being impressed by its curious distrust of itself—its apparently ineradicable tendency to abandon its whole philosophy at the first sign of strain. I need not point to what happens invariably in democratic states when the national safety is menaced. All the great tribunes of democracy, on such occasions, convert themselves, by a process as simple as taking a deep breath, into despots of an almost fabulous ferocity.

What Mencken was doing, in effect, was reasserting the snobbery of the Eastern Brahmins against the influence of Western-style democracy. For almost a century the man of superior intellectual ability had been made to feel guilty, but now it was time for him to come out of exile and take a position of leadership. Without the guidance of his wisdom, the American dream might very well go berserk. The frightening thing, as we look back at the twenties, is that that was just what was happening. The newly arrived middle class was spending its recent accumulation of wealth in a frenzy: the American dream of salvation and prosperity for the common man was fulfilled. Buy, buy, buy was the order of the day; and if you haven't cash, credit will do. Mencken grew so exasperated with this upsurge in the power of the little man, he decided to rewrite the Declaration of Independence as it might have been done if the Founding Fathers lived in the Jazz Age. The opening phrases go:

> When things get so balled up that the people of a country got to cut loose from some other country, and go it on their own hook, without asking no permission from nobody, excepting maybe God Almighty, then they ought to let everybody know why they done it, so that everybody can see they are not trying to put nothing over on nobody.

> All we got to say on this proposition is this: first, me and you is as good as anybody else, and maybe a damn sight better; second, nobody ain't got no right to take away none of our rights; third, every man has got a right to live, to come and go as he pleases, and to have a good time whichever way he likes. . . .

While Mencken was hurling his shafts in essay form, other writers were converting similar beliefs into imaginative fiction. Scott Fitzgerald recorded the intense anxiety, frustration, and terror underlying the frolic of the Roaring Twenties. Ernest Hemingway reflected the impotence of the men and women of postwar Europe and America. Theodore Dreiser carried the Realism of the turn of the century to the summit of tragedy.

Dreiser was one of several writers whose description of Western values contrasted sharply with the West humorists of the previous century knew. The shock wave radiating from the closing of the frontier was now rolling over the consciousness of all our writers. Whereas before the West was the land of promise and the home of fulfillment, it now seemed to be a repository for the worst in American culture: anti-intellectualism, the love of mediocrity, the worship of tastelessness. Sherwood Anderson saw the typical resident of a small Ohio town as a "grotesque," and Sinclair Lewis's characterization of the Midwesterner left us with the word Babbitt. The West was no longer the source of our best humor: it was now the object of it. Addressing the citizens of the midwestern town of Zenith, George Babbitt described the West's Ideal Citizen—not exactly a Davy Crockett or a Mike Fink:

> I picture him first and foremost as being busier than a bird-dog, not wasting a lot of good time in daydreaming or going

to sassiety teas or kicking about things that are none of his business, but putting the zip into some store or profession or art. At night he lights up a good cigar, and climbs into the little old 'bus, and maybe cusses the carburetor, and shoots out home. He mows the lawn, or sneaks in some practice putting, and then he's ready for dinner. After dinner he tells the kiddies a story, or takes the family to the movies, or plays a few fists of bridge, or reads the evening paper, and a chapter or two of some good lively Western novel if he has a taste for literature, and maybe the folks next-door drop in and they sit and visit about their friends and topics of the day. Then he goes happily to bed, his conscience clear, having contributed his mite to the prosperity of the city and to his own bank-account.

Will Rogers, the homespun humorist, on stage in New York.

It is amusing to note that Babbitt was so far from his own Western heritage that he found it necessary to rediscover it through Western novels. There was one Westerner of the twenties, however, who kept the tradition of frontier wisdom very much alive. He was a genuine cowboy, and perhaps the best reason why he had managed to keep his identity is that he hailed from Oklahoma, one of the last states to be admitted to the union. His name was Will Rogers.

Rogers was not so much a writer as a lecturer and storyteller. His first two collections of sayings, published in 1919, were sayings and jokes, bits and gags he had used in his *Ziegfeld Follies* and *Midnight Frolic* acts. From then on he did columns and commentaries for a number of newspapers and magazines, including the *New York Times* and the *Saturday Evening Post.* In 1925 he began a column for the McNaught Syndicate called "The Worst Story I've Heard Today," and for two years he entertained readers daily with his versions of local, domestic or national news items. He also published in the *Times* a daily cable from Europe under the heading "Will Rogers Says." His death in 1935 in a plane accident deprived the nation of the last genuine folk humorist in a chain reaching back to Nathaniel Ward and his *Simple Cobler.*

Rogers loved his country passionately, and bore no hatreds—just peeves, the wry complaints of an essentially happy man. But that didn't blunt the edge of his complaints. He scarcely opened his mouth or put pen to paper without expressing an American criticism more sharply than any man of his time. Some random samples:

Now if there is one thing that we do worse than any other nation, it is try and manage somebody else's affairs.

It will take America fifteen years steady taking care of our own business and letting everybody else's alone to get us back to where everybody speaks to us again.

We will never get anywhere with our finances till we pass a law saying that every time we appropriate something we got to pass another bill along with it stating where the money is coming from.

Every time we have an election, we get in worse men and the country keeps right on going. Times have proven only one thing and that is you can't ruin this country, ever, with politics.

When a Gentleman [of Congress] quoted me on the floor the other day, another member took exception and said he objected to the remarks of a Professional Joke-Maker going into the Congressional Record. Now can you beat that for jealousy among people in the same line? Calling me a Professional Joke-Maker! He is right about everything but the Professional. They are the professional Joke Makers. I could study all my life and not think up half the amount of funny things they can think of in one Session of Congress. Besides my jokes don't do anybody any harm. You don't have to pay any attention to them. But every one of the jokes those birds makes is a law and hurts somebody, *generally everybody.*

Whether you looked at America's extraordinary growth in the twenties with tolerant amusement, as Rogers did, or with dour misgivings, as Mencken did, one thing was certain: the economy was inflating far faster than our ability to understand or control it. Many investors, large and small, had purchased goods, services and securities with tiny down payments, leaving the balance payable later on. America seemed to be afloat on a sea of credit. Believing that the happy situation would go on forever, no one listened to warnings that if too many people wanted to call in their debts at the same time, it could start a chain reaction leading to the utter collapse of our economic system. It led Will Rogers to observe that "A debt is just as hard for a government to pay as for an individual. No debt ever came due at a good time. Borrowing is the only thing that is handy all the time."

On the October day in 1929 on which the stock market tumbled, America realized that its debt had come due.

10

The Flowering of American Humor

WILL ROGERS HAS SAID, "AS OUR GOVERNMENT DETERIORATES our humor increases." His statement might serve as the slogan of the 1930's. It wasn't exactly the government that had deteriorated—just everything else. Not since the Civil War had our way of life been so thoroughly disrupted; yet never, before or after, did we laugh so much.

The collapse of the stock market is regarded as one of the most momentous events of modern history. Few single moments had created such a violent change in the political, economic, and cultural life of a nation. The soundness of our government; the supreme self-confidence of the nation's financial leaders; the seemingly limitless abundance of raw material, farm products, and labor;

the certainty of tomorrow's wage or salary; the apparently infinite availability of credit; the endless good times—all seemed to burst like overinflated balloons, as the same dynamic principle that had inflated the economy over a ten-year period deflated it within a few days. The effects were felt immediately by the big financiers and industrialists, but within a short time men at the bottom were touched as hundreds of thousands of workers were laid off their jobs to enable their bosses to recover their balance. The government, led first by Hoover and then by Roosevelt, took an active role in trying to restore pre-Depression soundness, but it would take years before any kind of stability could be established.

Many historians have expressed great wonder that in the midst of the severest setback this nation has ever suffered, a time of bleakest despair, American humor should choose its time to come of age. But both because of our hopelessness and in spite of it, literary laughter echoed through the United States as it had not done since the days before the Civil War. Yet the humor of the thirties exceeded even those times with its variety, ingenuity, and sophistication.

It would be interesting to wonder whether the army of humorists who paraded into prominence in the thirties would have been as successful as they were if no Depression existed. It seems unlikely. The catastrophe registered on their imaginations in a special way. For they had come of age in fairly good times. The sudden and overwhelming specter of poverty in the midst of so much wealth, of sadness where only a short time ago had been joy, of bewilderment in place of cockiness, sharpened their sense of the ironic. Irony, as the Greeks had concluded, is the highest form of humor because, in depicting how the mighty are trapped by their own snares, it is close to tragedy. And so in the tragedy suffered by the mightiest nation the globe had ever borne was a lesson in high humor, and happily for us, a battalion of geniuses were on hand to take advantage of it. Perhaps some of them remembered what Lincoln had said under the strain of war: "If I did not laugh I should die."

What made these writers different was their diversity of background. They came from all points of the compass, and though their regions gave their wit special flavor, there was no consideration of North vs. South or East vs. West. These traditional rivals, faced with a common crisis, dropped their hostilities and united to face it. The intelligentsia took on some of the rough spontaneity of the frontier humorist; and the old frontier type, dropping his distrust of Eastern snobbery, emerged with a liking for the sparkle of high culture. This new composite of the best qualities of East and West addressed itself to an increasingly urban and sophisticated audience, so that its brilliance reflected back on itself like a roomful of crystal. Magazines like *The New Yorker*, *Saturday Evening Post*, and *Colliers* competed hotly to represent the new kind of writing, the new kind of attitude, the new kind of American.

What welded these writers together was the same thing that welded all Americans together: the realization that there were some things beyond the control of the individual. The war and the stock market disaster had taught us that the fates of nations are beyond the power of any single human being to decide. On the contrary, the individual was a victim of social forces. The myth of the Western hero, a man alone against the elements and Indians and bad men, had been one by which *all* Americans lived, for all had believed that by their own little vote they could alter the course of their country. But the myth had been dissolving for a long time, and the Crash finally put an end to it. Ogden Nash, poet laureate of the age, captured this loss of faith in the individual in a poem entitled "Election Day Is a Holiday":

People on whom I do not bother to dote
Are people who do not bother to vote.
Heaven forbid that they should ever be exempt
From contumely, obloquy and various kinds of contempt.
Some of them like Toscanini and some like Rudy Vallée,
But all of them take about as much interest in their right to ballot as their right to ballet.
They haven't voted since the heyday of Miss Russell (Lillian)
And excuse themselves by saying What's the difference of one vote in fifty million? . . .

With few exceptions the Western hero was now at best a member of the middle class like everyone else, or at worst a seedy yokel driven to desperation by economic hardship, drought and dust, and the loss of self-respect. The American dream had been riding on the triumph of the Western hero, and out of the shattering of the dream would come a new figure. Literary critics would call him an "anti-hero."

More and more, we would see him as the protagonist of twentieth-century humor. He was the product of the futile struggle of the average man with the frustrating complexity of modern life. He knew that it was senseless to try controlling the great forces of the Industrial Age, so

Charlie Chaplin exemplified the average man struggling with the complexity of modern life.

he concentrated on the little ones. That he usually lost even those fights wasn't important; at least he was fighting, and his foe was visible and understandable and vulnerable. Whether you won or lost, a battle with an auto engine was a lot more satisfying than one with something vaguely called "economic reversals."

Because the Industrial Revolution had churned up so many problems for modern man, the variety of subjects dealt with by the new generation of humorists was tremendous. The only rule they were pledged to observe was not to deal with anything important. Political or religious themes, which had provided themes for the great wits of bygone eras, were off-limits. "Keep it light" were the words on their banners as they plunged, with mighty broadswords swinging, into warfare against an army of midgets. If they did tackle something grandiose, it was with tongue thrust deeply into cheek, as Robert Benchley did in *How to Understand International Finance*:

> Now there is a certain principle which has to be followed in all financial discussions involving sums over one hundred dollars. There is probably not more than one hundred dollars in actual cash in circulation today. That is, if you were to call in all the bills and silver and gold in the country at noon tomorrow and pile them up on the table, you would find that you had just about one hundred dollars, with perhaps several Canadian pennies and a few peppermint life-savers. All the rest of the money you hear about doesn't exist. It is conversation money. When you hear of a transaction involving $50,000,000 it means that one firm wrote "$50,000,000" on a piece of paper and gave it to another firm. . . .

And so authors like Nash, Benchley, James Thurber, S. J. Perelman, Dorothy Parker, E. B. White, Wolcott

Gibbs, Frank Sullivan, Ring Lardner, Corey Ford, William Saroyan, Damon Runyon, George S. Kaufman, and Alexander Woollcott, with varying degrees of wistfulness or irascibility, amusement or bewilderment, took on the innovations of modern living. But no matter how distinctly they differed from each other in the way they expressed it, they all were pretty much agreed on this: that no matter what kind of machinery they drove around in, heard the news on, or vacuumed their rugs with—people were still people. Progress had not made a dent in human nature.

James Thurber, for example, had grown accustomed to his friend's simple rural telephone number, 905 Ring 4. He woke up one day to learn that it had been changed to New Milford 1006 W–1. His *friend* was still the same, but life had been made maddeningly worse by this technological "improvement." What kind of man perpetrates such "progress," he wonders:

> Lots worse things have happened to me, but not many that I keep thinking about more often. I have slowly built up in my mind a picture of the official in Hartford who thought up that change. His name, as it comes to me in dreams, is Rudwooll Y. Peffifoss. Peffifoss, who has had to go through a lot of hell, not only on account of the name Peffifoss, but also on account of Rudwooll (the Y is for Yurmurm), has had to compensate for what has happened to him in this life. Working up relentlessly and maliciously to an important post in the Number Changing Department of the Connecticut Telephone Company, he has decided to get back at the world for what he conceives it has done to him. He spends the day going through phone books looking for simple, easily remembered numbers like 905 Ring 4, and when he finds one, he claps his hands and calls his secretary, a Miss Rettig.

> "Take a number change, Miss Rettig," he says with an evil smile. "New Milford 905 Ring 4 to be changed to Pussymeister W–7 Oh 8 0h 9 6 J–4."

Thurber's genius reached its peak in his story "The Secret Life of Walter Mitty," a narration of the fantasy life of the classic anti-hero. Mitty is a middle-class weakling devoid of heroic qualities. But when he imagines himself a surgeon, a navy commander, or an attorney for the defense, he soars to heights of gallantry and skill. Then he is yanked back to the reality of a nagging wife and municipal traffic:

> Walter Mitty stopped the car in front of the building where his wife went to have her hair done. "Remember to get those overshoes while I'm having my hair done," she said. "I don't need overshoes," said Mitty. She put her mirror back into her bag. "We've been through all that," she said, getting out of the car. "You're not a young man any longer." He raced the engine a little. "Why don't you wear your gloves? Have you lost your gloves?" Walter Mitty reached in a pocket and brought out the gloves. He put them on, but after she had turned and gone into the building and he had driven on to a red light, he took them off again. "Pick it up, brother!" snapped a cop as the light changed, and Mitty hastily pulled on his gloves and lurched ahead. He drove around the streets aimlessly for a time, and then he drove past the hospital on his way to the parking lot.
>
> . . . "It's the millionaire banker, Wellington McMillan," said the pretty nurse. "Yes?" said Walter Mitty, removing his gloves slowly. "Who has the case?"

Here was the anti-hero, the poor soul, the schnook, the loser, in all his non-glory.

For sidesplitting characterization of such a loser, no one could top Robert Benchley. Rarely in history has one man been shoved, stepped on, put upon, discomfited and abused in so many ways as he was. You would think that society had been placed on earth with the specific purpose of making him miserable—and that is just what he wanted you to think.

Benchley simply couldn't walk five paces or stand still for ten seconds without finding something puzzling, confusing, or distressing. When he went to the bank he realized that it is impossible to pick up thin coins on the marble counter in front of the teller's window. When he accepted a poker invitation it was to discover that instead of the straightforward game he'd expected, they were playing such variations as hayfever (one card up, two down, the last two up, one-eyed jacks, sevens and nines wild, high-low), or Whistle Up Your Windpipe (seven-card stud, first and last cards up, deuces, threes, and red-haired queens wild, high-low-and-medium), and others like Breezy-Weezy and Mice Afloat. He could find the *darndest* things to wonder about, as his essay "Call for Mr. Kenworthy!" illustrates—yet they were the same things *we* wonder about but dismiss as part of the incomprehensible process of modern living:

> A great many people have wondered to themselves, in print, just where the little black laundry studs go after they have been yanked from the shirt. Others pass this by as inconsequential, but are concerned over the ultimate disposition of all the pencil stubs that are thrown away. Such futile rumination is all well enough for those who like it. As for me, give me a big, throbbing question like this: "Who are the people that one hears being paged in hotels? Are they real people or are they decoys? And if they are real people, what are they being paged for?"

Benchley may have been speaking for everybody when he concluded, in another sketch called "The Real Public Enemies," that "animate enemies"—"people who set out with a definite idea in their minds of getting me"—were not to be feared as much as inanimate:

> It is the inanimate enemies who have me baffled. The hundred and one little bits of wood and metal that go to make up the impedimenta of our daily life—the shoes and pins, the picture books and door keys, the bits of fluff and sheets of newspaper—each and every one with just as much vicious ill-will toward me personally as the meanest footpad who roams the streets, each and every one bent on my humiliation and working together, as on one great team, to bedevil and confuse me and to get me into a neurasthenics' home before I am sixty. I can't fight these boys. They've got me licked.

S. J. Perelman, though not quite so submissive in his acceptance of malevolent fate as Benchley and Thurber, nevertheless found himself constantly on the losing side of the ledger. But that didn't stop him from getting up to fulminate brilliantly on every conceivable annoyance, inconvenience, and imposition modern life had to offer. Such as "Insert Flap 'A' and Throw Away":

> One stifling summer afternoon last August, in the attic of a tiny stone house in Pennsylvania, I made a most interesting discovery: the shortest, cheapest method of inducing a nervous breakdown ever perfected. In this technique (eventually adopted by the psychology department of Duke University, which will adopt anything), the subject is placed in a sharply sloping attic heated to 340° F. and given a mothproof closet known as the Jiffy-Cloz to assemble. The Jiffy-Cloz, procurable at any department store or neigh-

> borhood insane asylum, consists of half a dozen gigantic sheets of red cardboard, two plywood doors, a clothes rack, and a packet of staples. With these is included a set of instructions mimeographed in pale-violet ink, fruity with phrases like "Pass Section F through Slot AA, taking care not to fold tabs behind washers (See Fig. 9)." The cardboard is so processed that as the subject struggles convulsively to force the staple through, it suddenly buckles, plunging the staple deep into his thumb. He thereupon springs up with a dolorous cry and smites his knob (Section K) on the rafters (RR).

Despite the popularity of such anti-heroism, the need for a glamorous protagonist to root for runs deep in our souls. While it was pleasurable to identify with losers, Americans still sought the familiar red-blooded, old-fashioned, bigger-than-life type. They found him in several fields. One was nostalgia. Though we know when we think about it that the past was never as ideal as we remember it, many writers looked back to the times of their parents and grandparents for refuge from current troubles. Remembrances of Irish, Jewish, Italian, Scandinavian, and other immigrant groups, so rich in dialect, began to flourish. And standing for all of them was Clarence Day, author of *Life With Father* and *Life With Mother*. From the former comes this excerpt, which could perhaps represent America itself looking back at a time when its own ledgers were neatly kept and balanced:

> Father was always trying to make Mother keep track of the household expenses. He was systematic by nature and he had had a sound business training. He had a full set of account books at home in addition to those in his office—a personal cashbook, journal, and ledger—in which he carefully made double entries. His home ledger showed at a

> glance exactly how much a month or a year his clothes or his clubs or his cigar bills amounted to. . . .
>
> Every once in so often he tried to explain his system to Mother. But his stout, leather-bound ledgers, and his methodical ruling of lines in red ink, and the whole business of putting down every little expense every day, were too much for her. . . .

Another place where we found our heroes was sports. The immense growth in popularity of professional baseball, football, and other sports resulted in intense worship of sports stars like Babe Ruth, Lou Gehrig, and Red Grange. Still another was crime. Despite their better judgment, many Americans were compelled to admire the violent exploits of crime czars of the 1920's and 1930's because such men, like the frontiersmen of old, defied the Establishment. In an age when "the system" had defeated so many, it was gratifying to see *someone* beating it.

These forms of hero-worship produced a satirical literature in the 1930's that enjoyed itself at the expense of the heroes. An important feature of the frontier democratic tradition was distrust and jealousy of anyone who became too important, as we have seen. Writers of the time eventually turned their weapons on the athlete and the criminal. Ring Lardner was among the leading satirists of the sports scene, while Damon Runyon developed a unique literature that made the criminal so sympathetic we might be tempted to classify him as a loser. "Hold 'Em, Yale!," a Runyon story bringing together the elements of sports and crime opens in this fashion:

> What I am doing in New Haven on the day of a very large football game between the Harvards and the Yales is some-

> thing which calls for quite a little explanation, because I am not such a guy as you will expect to find in New Haven at any time, and especially on the day of a large football game. But there I am, and the reason I am there goes back to a Friday night when I am sitting in Mindy's restaurant on Broadway thinking of very little except how I can get hold of a few potatoes to take care of the old overhead. And while I am sitting there, who comes in but Sam the Gonoph, who is a ticket speculator by trade, and who seems to be looking all around and about.
>
> Well, Sam the Gonoph gets to talking to me, and it turns out he is looking for a guy by the name of Gigolo Georgie, who is called Gigolo Georgie because he is always hanging about night clubs wearing a little mustache and white spats, and dancing with old dolls. In fact, Gigolo Georgie is nothing but a gentleman bum, and I am surprised that Sam the Gonoph is looking for him.

But while athletes and racketeers were bringing Americans the vicarious thrill of identifying with an old-fashioned hero, another type was even more successful: the movie star.

It was not entirely at random that Hollywood, rather than other cities active in the industry like New York and Chicago, became the home of the film. As we have seen, the American dream of land, freedom, and a second chance to achieve redemption, depended on the westward movement of the frontier. A crisis in our sense of humor occurred when the nation reached the western border of expansion, the Pacific Ocean. The Hollywood community, however, was able to extend the frontier into a new dimension through motion pictures. Hollywood performed the invaluable service of keeping alive our most cherished hopes at a time when they were taking terrible punishment. But that is not to say we didn't pay for the service.

However exciting movies are to us today, it is difficult to describe how meaningful they were to the people living in Depression days. Deprived of their material wealth, they embraced the fantasy and romance, the danger, the intrigue, the heroism, and the violence of films as if they were the real thing. The motion picture industry became not just an artistic medium, but a process for manufacturing dreams. Hollywood was becoming a place where America's confusion between real life and imagined life focussed. Acted roles and life roles of movie stars got jumbled up in the minds of fans, and eventually in the minds of the stars themselves. Like medieval architects, the members of the Hollywood "colony" were erecting a fortress dedicated to preventing intrusion of ugly truths like poverty, uncleanliness, failure, the Depression, and European rearmament. It was the old isolationism in a new form, and in exporting this product into the minds of millions of Americans, Hollywood was perpetuating a dangerous state of mind. To counter this tendency, a large number of writers who had gone through the movie-making mills tried to reveal some of the hard realities about the fantastic world on the West Coast, and to warn Americans that their investment in the dream world of the film was as unhealthy as their investment in the stock market had been in the previous decade. Some of the satire was bitter, as we see in this passage from a Nathaniel West novel, *Miss Lonelyhearts*, describing the fans and curiosity seekers crowding outside a Hollywood premiere:

All their lives they had slaved at some kind of dull, heavy

labor, behind desks and counters, in the field and at tedious machines of all sorts, saving their pennies and dreaming of the leisure that would be theirs when they had enough. Finally that day came. They would draw a weekly income of ten or fifteen dollars. Where else should they go but California, the land of sunshine and oranges?

Once there, they discovered that sunshine isn't enough. They get tired of oranges, even of avocado pears and passion fruit. Nothing happens. They don't know what to do with their time. They haven't the mental equipment for leisure, the money nor the physical equipment for pleasure. Did they slave so long just to go on an occasional Iowa picnic? What else is there? They watch the waves come in at Venice. There wasn't any ocean where most of them came from, but after you've seen one wave, you've seen them all. The same is true of the airplanes at Glendale. If only a plane would crash once in a while so that they could watch the passengers being consumed in a "holocaust of flame," as the newspapers put it. But the planes never crash. . . .

Far more easygoing about Hollywood was S. J. Perelman. Called there to write film scripts, he recalls in an essay, "Strictly from Hunger," his first experience in the movie capital:

The violet hush of twilight was descending over Los Angeles as my hostess, Violet Hush, and I left its suburbs headed toward Hollywood. In the distance a glow of huge piles of burning motion-picture scripts lit up the sky. The crisp tang of frying writers and directors whetted my appetite. How good it was to be alive, I thought, inhaling deep lungfuls of carbon monoxide. Suddenly our powerful Gatti-Cazazza slid to a stop in the traffic.

"What is it, Jenkin?" Violet called anxiously through the speaking-tube to the chauffeur (played by Lyle Talbot).

A *suttee* was in progress by the roadside, he said—did we wish to see it? Quickly Violet and I elbowed our way through the crowd. An enormous funeral pyre composed of thousands of feet of film and scripts, drenched with Chanel Number 5, awaited the torch of Jack Holt, who was to act as master of ceremonies. In a few terse words Violet explained this unusual custom borrowed from the Hindus and never paid for. The worst disgrace that can befall a producer is an unkind notice from a New York reviewer. He is shunned by his friends, thrown into bankruptcy, and like a Japanese electing hara-kiri, he commits suttee. A great bonfire is made of the film, and the luckless producer, followed by directors, actors, technicians and the producer's wives, immolate themselves.

The laughter of the 1930's linked us to the laughter of a century before. The American settler, discovering a land and an experience altogether new, had laughed innocently with the enchantment of nature. Now, Americans were discovering a new kind of land, a land of electricity and mechanics, of industry and mass media, and their bewilderment with it brought on almost the same kind of innocent laughter as their frontier ancestors had known. The frontier was gone, but not the spirit that had built it.

The glory of the Depression is that it brought out one of the great traits of the American character: the ability to laugh in the face of terrible hardship. In a profoundly troubled time, it carried us through the darkness. A population deprived of its material wealth refused to release its clutch on the other kind of wealth that had made us an unconquerable people: our pride, our dignity, and, above all, our sense of humor.

11
War Again

ALTHOUGH THE AMERICAN ECONOMY WAS BEGINNING TO recover from the Depression, it took a worldwide war to boost it into full productivity. With Germany's tentacles reaching out across Europe in the late thirties to gather in country after country, American attention turned to the possibility of involvement. The isolationist attitude prevailed again, for so much remained to be done for our own suffering population that we could hardly be expected to rescue someone else's. Yet our moral indignation over Nazi aggressions, our sympathy for the European victims, and a realization that war preparations might stimulate our economic system, began pushing us towards commitment. The attack on Pearl Harbor caught us shamefully unprepared, but the stupendous vigor with which Americans dedicated themselves to the war effort shows how eager they had been to have a cause that would unite all the elements of our ailing society.

American entrance into the hostilities brought forth a splendid effort on the part of the comics too. The wit that had carried their country through the Depression now turned toward keeping up the spirits both of the troops and the folks back home. Many writers worked for *Stars & Stripes* and other military publications dedicated to the lighter side of service life. Comedians like Bob Hope tirelessly toured the front, bringing gales of laughter to soldiers by cracking jokes about unpleasant conditions (including the officers) that men in uniform would not have dared to attempt. Hope selflessly toured hospitals, cheering wounded men with quips like "Okay fellows, don't get up!"; "You'll do anything to avoid the draft"; and "Did you see the show this evening, or were you already sick?" Possibly the funniest one-liner of the war was attributed to Groucho Marx. Picking up a ringing phone in an officer's quarters, he answered "Hello, this is World War Two." Reporters from the front found much to amuse them among the sordid episodes they witnessed. A. J. Liebling, for example, passed to his home publication this gem of an exchange:

> "Give da passwoy," I once heard a First Division sentinel challenge.
>
> "Nobody told me nuttin," the challenged soldier replied.
>
> "What outfitchas outuv?"
>
> "Foy Signals."
>
> "Whynchas get on da ball? Da Passwoy is 'tached roof.' "
>
> "What is it mean?"
>
> "How do I know? Whaddya tink I yam, da Quiz Kids?"

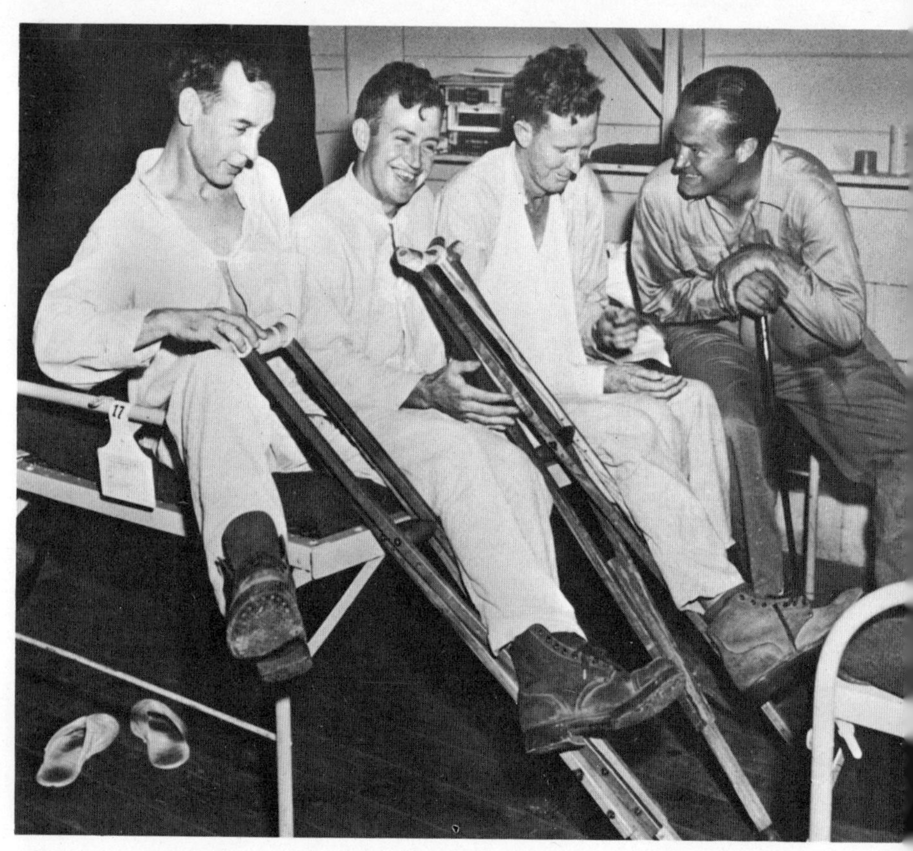

Bob Hope toured the front, cheering wounded men with his quips.

Meanwhile, back on the home front, the quickly grown medium of radio was making a vital contribution. Comedians like Fred Allen and Jack Benny were converting conditions like rationing and blackouts into the weapons of wit, just as armament manufacturers converted tin cans into guns. When New York City dwellers were ordered to keep their lights dim to subdue the threat of enemy bombers, Fred Allen interviewed for his audience a character, played of course by an actor, named "Sharp Sherman":

Allen: What is your work?

Sherman: Work is a sucker's pastime, chum. I live by my wits . . .

Allen: How do you get by?

Sherman: Rackets, chum. I keep 'em up to the minute . . .

Allen: What about this dim-out, Sherman?

Sherman: I got a coupla gimmicks operatin' already, chum.

Allen: What gimmicks?

Sherman: I got a dim-out Racin' Form.

Allen: What is that?

Sherman: Hundreds of horseplayers used to stand in front of restaurants and read their Racin' Forms by the light of the restaurant windows. Today, them windows is dimmed out.

Allen: Oh, and your—

Sherman: My Racin' Form's got a lightnin' bug tied on it. A horseplayer can read it anyplace.

Allen: What is your other dim-out gimmick?

Sherman: I'm light-leggin'.

Allen: What is light-legging?

Sherman: It's like bootleggin' only with a light . . . I nudge you and say, "Can you use a little light, chum?"

The economies practiced by American citizens during the war years are amusingly represented by a description by E. B. White, in a collection entitled *Quo Vadimus?*, of an operation he underwent in Boston:

Because of the war the situation in hospitals is, of course, serious. A civilian feels embarrassed to be there at all, occupying valuable space and wasting the time and strength of the nurses, the student nurses, the nurses' aides, and the Gray Ladies. But I discovered that there is a new spirit in hospitals which, in its own way, is as merciful and resolute as the old, and every bit as mad. A patient, when he enters, receives a booklet reminding him that hospitals are shorthanded and asking him not to bother the nurses unnecessarily. If he is a person of any conscience, he takes this quite literally, resolving not to push his call switch unless he is bleeding to death or the room is on fire. . . .

As for routine chores, I did them myself, for the most part. Each morning I arose from bed and went at the room, tidying it up and doing all the dozens of things that need doing in an early-morning sickroom. First I would get down and crawl under the bed to retrieve the night's accumulation of blood-soaked paper handkerchiefs, which formed a dismal ring around the scrap basket where I had missed my aim in the dark. . . . One morning, in one of those passionate fits of neatness which overwhelm me from time to time, I spent an hour or so on my hands and knees, clearing the room of bobby pins left by a former occupant.

Many humorists were too busy fighting or otherwise serving and could not record their impressions until after the war. But their stories and books were well worth waiting for. Such memorable products as *Mr. Roberts* and *No Time for Sergeants* reminded us that war does have a lighter side. Most such books revolved around some snafu or another—the word "Snafu" meaning Situation Normal, All Fouled Up. Because Americans were not a militaristic people, the foul-ups of a military operation rarely failed to tickle them—just as they had tickled Mark Twain. A typical example comes from the pen of Mac Hyman in *No Time for Sergeants:*

> Anyhow, I woke up and felt the plane going in these big circles, and then I looked over to the desk and there was Lieutenant Bridges standing holding one of the maps in his hand and looking at it, and Lieutenant Cover arguing with him, rattling papers around and trying to show him how he had figured this and that. Lieutenant Kendall was setting over there watching them with his chin propped up on his hands, and Lieutenant Gardell was up front flying the plane in these big circles, looking around every once in awhile to see what was going on with the big cigar stuck out of his mouth; they was talking loud and everybody seemed real interested in it, and it seemed like Lieutenant Bridges knowed a lot about navigation himself even though he was the pilot. He was waving the map around saying, "I don't care what your figures show. I guess I can look out the window and *see,* can't I?"

Had the war ended as the First World War had, the postwar period might have resembled that of the 1920's —prosperous, optimistic, expansive. But two events made it, instead, a time of unmitigated tension, turning what might have been a joyous period of rebuilding and brotherhood into one of terror more gripping than any thing the world had ever known. The first was the confrontation between the Russian and American armies along the collapsing German front. The second was the dropping of the atomic bombs on Hiroshima and Nagasaki. The major powers, instead of withdrawing to former boundaries, occupied conquered territory and faced off for a prolonged Cold War.

Thus, the mood in the late 1940's was bitterness sharper than anything felt by the American expatriates in Paris after the First World War. Not only were we disgusted with having had to shed our blood a second time in less than thirty years; we were appalled to see that new war preparations were following on the coattails of our peace treaties. And those preparations were so deadly that the prospect of a Third World War was equivalent to doomsday. Hydrogen warheads had not yet been developed; and Russia was not to explode its own atomic bombs for some years to come. But it was obvious that Russia would soon develop nuclear capability, and both countries would refine these monstrous weapons. To a nation heartsick and weary of war, the future seemed almost unbearably depressing.

It is little wonder, then, that the postwar age saw an outbreak of what was to be called "sick" humor. It was born not just out of adversity, not just out of desperation even; it was the expression of utter futility. It was the humor of madmen. No indignity, no degradation, no victimization was off limits. The sick humorist believed at base that the world had gone mad; otherwise why would it pursue the very atrocities it claimed to abhor? Compared to that kind of madness, any private kind would seem sane.

And so a kind of mock-madness came to characterize the humor of the 1950's and early 1960's. It pretended to have no values at all. Publications like *Mad* magazine, movies like *Dr. Strangelove, or How I Learned to Stop Worrying and Love the Bomb*, comedians like Lenny Bruce sprang up, all excusing their violations of good taste on the grounds that no one could behave as insanely as the world itself was behaving. Actually their humor was not valueless at all: it was a radical protest against a humanity that was losing its values. Until society could control its brutality, it had no right to criticize anyone for finding brutality funny.

It was in the 1950's that the humor of the anti-hero began to reach a new high as the individual seemed even further from involvement with life than ever before. Alan Harrington, in his book, *The Revelations of Dr. Modesto,* satirized this alienation with a thirty-point program for destroying personality. A few of these:

> 1. Since your self grates on others, and makes you miserable, get rid of it.
>
> 2. In our society, in our time, it does not pay to be yourself. People laugh at you and call you strange—even if it was your father's fault.
>
> 3. Look around you, and see who is the happy man. He is the one Just Like Everybody Else. "Oh, so that is the way to be?" you ask, and I say, yes, that is the way you and I must be.
>
> 4. You are a sensitive person in a world of Brutes. Like a feeble animal, you need protective coloration. You must hide.
>
> 5. The only place to hide is in the center of their culture. Be more average than anyone!

The themes of impotence, inadequacy, and ineffectiveness, used by serious writers of the time, carried over into comic literature as well. The psychiatrist, representing sane reality, became the butt of much humor, for sane reality wasn't sane at all. Cartoonists like Jules Feiffer portrayed man's paralysis in an age when there was no one to turn to for guidelines on what was sick and what was healthy. A typical analyst, like this one devised by Roger Price in *In One Head and Out the Other,* seemed worse off than his patients:

When a new patient consults Dr. Dorsey, the procedure is as follows. After a preliminary examination of the patient's Heredity, Social Attitudes, Marital Status, and Suit Pockets, Dr. Dorsey tells him to go home and write a complete history of his own life, putting in every detail, no matter how embarrassing or libelous. The patient does this and returns in a few days with the history. Dr. Dorsey then reads the patient's history, corrects the grammar as best he can, changes a few names around, and submits it to *True Story Magazine*.

One of the most representative books came at the end of this era: *Catch-22* by Joseph Heller, from which the following key passage is taken:

Outside the hospital the war was still going on. Men went mad and were rewarded with medals. All over the world, boys on every side of the bomb line were laying down their lives for what they had been told was their country, and no one seemed to mind, least of all the boys who were laying down their young lives. . . .

But Yossarian couldn't be happy. . . . because outside the hospital there was still nothing funny going on. The only thing going on was a war, and no one seemed to notice but Yossarian and Dunbar. And when Yossarian tried to remind people, they drew away from him and thought *he* was crazy. Even Clevinger, who should have known better but didn't, had told him he was crazy the last time they had seen each other, which was just before Yossarian had fled into the hospital.

Clevinger stared at him with apoplectic rage and indignation, and, clawing the table with both hands, had shouted, "You're crazy!"

"Clevinger, what do you want from people?" Dunbar had replied warily above the noise of the officers' club.

"I'm not joking," Yossarian persisted.

"They're not trying to kill you," Clevinger cried.

"Then why are they shooting at me?" Yossarian asked.

"They're shooting at *everyone,*" Clevinger answered. "They're trying to kill everyone."

"And what difference does that make?"

Yossarian, on the surface of it, sounded a little crazy. But actually he was trying to make us realize that war, especially in the atomic age, denied the sanctity of the individual. If we weren't to doom ourselves, we would have to stop thinking of man as a statistic. The human race was still, as it always had been, composed of billions of distinct, irreplaceable individuals.

But most people could take little comfort from such reassertions of belief in the individual. The civilization of the early atomic age, helpless before doomsday weaponry, lived very near the verge of hysteria, gripped by the fear that a madman might be tempted to press the button that would blast human life from the earth. Is it any wonder that our standards of propriety in sex and violence in literature were lowered? With annihilation so near at hand, what good were standards of propriety?

Not all writers of the era were charged with the impulse to abandon old values. Some were content to trust to God and to the wisdom of man; others tried to make believe The Bomb didn't exist, or reasoned there was nothing they could do about it. These writers reflected our attempts to return to the commonplace task of earning a living and providing for a family and future. As the Cold War began to warm just a little, men began to feel they might be able to dream again.

For a great part of the American population the dream took the form of a longing for a piece of land and a home in the country, and thus began the great middle class exodus from cities to suburbs. This exodus provided a favorite theme for humorists as they saw ironic contrasts between this dream—a modern statement of the old frontier dream—and its fulfillment. In the suburbs you could find assembly-line conformity, mediocrity of taste, inconvenience and frustration. Was this the brave new world our forefathers had risked death to secure for us? It seemed as if the American dream had played a jolly good joke on the dreamers. S. J. Perelman was among the modern pioneers to discover it, as his book *Acres and Pains* attests:

> I began my career as a country squire with nothing but a high heart, a flask of citronella, and a fork for toasting marshmallows in case supplies ran low. In a scant fifteen years I have acquired a superb library of mortgages, mostly first editions, and the finest case of sacroiliac known to science. . . .
>
> When I first settled down on a heap of shale in the Delaware Valley, I too had a romantic picture of myself. For about a month I was a spare, sinewy frontiersman in fringed buckskin, with crinkly little lines about the eyes and a slow laconic drawl. One look told you that my ringing ax and long Kentucky rifle would take the forest in jigtime. In fact, as I stepped off the train, I overhead a native remark admiringly, "His ringing ax and long Kentucky rifle should tame the forest in jigtime."
>
> After I almost blew off a toe cleaning an air rifle, though, I decided I was more the honest rural type. I started wearing patched blue jeans, mopped my forehead with a red banana (I found out later it should have been a red bandanna), and crumbled bits of earth between my fingers to see whether it was friable enough. Friable enough for what I wasn't quite sure but I kept at it until my wife screamed like a banshee if I so much as picked up a clod. I never entered

my kitchen like a normal individual; I always stamped in roaring "Well, Mother, got plenty of vittles for the menfolk? Thrashin' sure makes a man hongry!"

Another writer who finds the suburbs fertile ground for humor is Peter DeVries. Typical of the zany characters who proliferate there is the one they call One, from a story entitled—strangely enough—"One":

> My first impression of Trenkle was the same as my last, and both were identical with all those that lay changelessly between: that of a man bent on talking in epigrams. He had a nickname he was completely oblivious of. Among ourselves, we who knew him never called him Trenkle, or Philip, either, which was his first name; we called him One, after the indefinite pronoun he constantly used—"One should always look at El Grecos on an empty stomach," and "Life is a carnival at which one should throw the balls at the prizes," and "There are types of innocence of which one should not be guilty," and so on.

Another outstanding recorder of suburban frustrations is H. Allen Smith. Although writing with a light hand, Smith realized that new cultural patterns were forming in the suburban movement, new values and codes, new dreams. In his delightful collection of essays, *Let the Crabgrass Grow*, he sets down in a mock-sociological manner some conclusions about that emerging type of frontiersman, the commuter:

> *CLASS DISTINCTIONS*
>
> Only two classes are recognized: those who ride in the smoking cars and those who ride elsewhere. The smoking car is primarily for rowdy people and the code does not apply to them. They are the talkers, the clowns, the card players, and the psychological misfits. They are not wanted in the

cars where the dignity of man prevails and they know it, and as a general thing they stay in their proper place.

CONVERSATION

All but forbidden. If there is any talk at all it should be limited to monosyllables. Two men may occupy the same seat every morning for ten years. They bury their faces in their newspapers and keep quiet. They never discuss the news, no matter how important it may be. . . .

OUTSIDE SOCIAL CONTACTS

Disapproved. These same two men who spend twelve and a half hours together each week may encounter each other in the local supermarket or drug store or tavern. They don't speak. It is permitted for one to nod pleasantly in recognition, although some commuters regard even nodding as presumptuous. . . .

Just what were these commuters commuting *to?* It seems, reading the humor of the fifties, that everyone was preoccupied with "communications," such as television, motion pictures, public relations, advertising, and publishing. There is an important reason for this.

New modes of communication represented our hope of striking out into new frontiers. The physical boundaries of our nation may have been reached, and the interior settled, but there were still intellectual and spiritual frontiers as yet uncrossed, as yet unapproached. The technical perfection of television especially had unleashed vast potential for creative minds, and if it could be harnessed it would be of the utmost benefit to humanity.

It cannot be said, with respect to American humor, that much potential was harnessed in the fifties. Television, like early movies, was a crude medium that seldom raised itself beyond vaudeville. Some of the vaudeville was pretty good, in the hands of Milton Berle, Jackie Gleason, Dean Martin and Jerry Lewis, and Sid Caesar, but they hardly touched the visual possibilities. Fred Allen, driven off the radio waves when his sponsors and audience turned to "the tube" instead, remarked in his book appropriately titled *Treadmill to Oblivion:*

> Comedy has changed with the coming of television. The radio listener saw nothing: he had to use his imagination. It was possible for each individual to enjoy the same program according to his intellectual level and his mental capacity. In radio, a writer could create any scene that the listener

Fred Allen and Jack Benny clown on radio, which depended on imagination rather than sets and props for its effect.

could picture mentally. In television a writer is restricted by the limitations imposed on him by the scenic designers and the carpenter. With the high cost of living and the many problems facing him in the modern world, all the poor man had left was his imagination. Television has taken that away from him.

"There was a certain type of imaginative comedy that could be written for, and performed on, only the radio," Allen concluded. "Television comedy is mostly visual and the most successful of comedians today are the disciples of the slapstick." There were, of course, exceptions, with playwrights like Paddy Chayevsky rendering intelligent, sensitive, and highly dramatic works for the new medium. But such works required time, and the cruel demands of weekly, daily, and hourly television exacted from aspiring writers material that could be churned out quickly. The result was the week-to-week situation comedy, a dim reflection of the potent dramas produced by writers taking their time to think about character and meaning. The growing thinness of material led Newton Minow, a prominent figure in the industry, to describe it as a "vast wasteland."

Perhaps, in the vast wasteland of television, the annoying noisiness and repetitiousness of advertising, and the hypocrisies of public relations, one could hardly find a sign of a Renaissance of American culture. But these media were young, and prone to the mistakes of youth. They still represented the vehicles by which our dreams *could* be fulfilled in the hands of the right men.

The task of the sixties would be to find the right men.

12

Today and Tomorrow

HOW CAN WE CHARACTERIZE THE HUMOR OF OUR OWN time, and what can we expect of it tomorrow?

The scientific and technological advances of the past twenty years are certainly the most significant aspects of twentieth-century life. We refer to our own time as the Scientific Age, the Atomic Age, the Jet Age. Many observers, harkening back to Henry Adams' fear that the dynamo was supplanting the cathedral, believe we have come to worship science as the source of our salvation. We look to heart transplants as the key to immortality; to breaking genetic codes for perfecting man's body and character; to progress in communications for enlightening the ignorant people of the world. In short, the frontier of today is scientific progress, progress into outer space, into the ocean deeps, into the mysteries of the cell and the atom.

But there are some who will not kneel at the altar, asking questions highly relevant to the future of humanity. Can human nature be improved scientifically? Can technology bring happiness? Does wisdom follow from the accumulation of information? Could tampering with environment bring the opposite results from those we hope for? Are we, in worshipping science, worshipping the Devil in disguise?

There is a body of people who have deep reservations about our progress. Among them are many humorists who continue, in modern dress, to make fun of the gap between that old dream of salvation and the reality of what we have actually achieved. The fact that we can fly ten times faster today than we could sixty years ago, for instance, has not pacified the fear of being airborne, as witness these thoughts by Jean Kerr, taken from her book *The Snake Has All the Lines*:

> I never bring reading material aboard a plane because I am convinced that if I'm not right there, alert every minute, keeping my eye on things, heaven knows what might happen to us. When it comes to selecting a seat I am torn between my wish to sit well back in the tail (surely the safest place to be when we crash) and the feeling that it is my civic duty to take a place next to the window where I can keep a constant watch over the engines. You have no idea how heedless and selfish some passengers are—reading magazines and munching sandwiches the while that I, alone, am keeping that plane aloft by tugging upward on the arms of my chair and concentrating intensely, sometimes for hours. And when it becomes absolutely clear that something is amiss, who has to ask that simple, straightforward question

that will clarify things? I do. Honestly, I don't think these people care whether they live or die.

Another favorite theme of contemporary humorists is the contrast between scientific investigation and plain common sense. While scientists strive mightily, draining the funds of great foundations and the energies of whole universities, to prove some remote thesis, the man in the street can reach the same conclusions effortlessly. Not long ago, after countless thousands of dollars had been spent developing a computerized machine that could pick out defective parts on an assembly line, someone demonstrated that the same job could be done by—pigeons! In *Let the Crabgrass Grow*, H. Allen Smith discusses weather prediction in these terms:

> The atomic bomb has superseded all other agencies as a blamable source of bad weather. The recent history of popular climatology in our section begins with the 1950 water famine in New York City, at which time a scientist was given an airplane and some dry ice and sent to seed clouds. His efforts to fill the city's reservoirs were not too successful but, in the opinion of a great many citizens, he fouled up the atmosphere over the whole Middle Atlantic seaboard. . . . Then he was rescued from all this abuse by the woolly bear.
>
> The woolly bear is a worm in a fur coat. Somebody decided that the disposition of the brown and black fur segments on the worm's body were a true indication of winter weather to come. People forgot the cloud-seeder, threw away their almanacs, and went hog-wild about woolly bears. That is, until the winter of 1952-1953. That autumn the fur on the worm foretold a long and brutal winter and everyone rushed out and bought extra weather-stripping and snow shovels and earmuffs, and then the winter turned out to be

extraordinarily temperate. It was, in fact, one of the mildest winters we've had in years. . . . Yet there had to be an explanation for the mild winter, and the sopping spring that followed, so now the nuclear fission theory of weather derangement began to pick up steam. . . .

I have heard that the Atomic Energy Commission has denied that it is responsible for eccentricities of the weather. I choose to go along with the sovereign people and their interpretation of Nature's capricious ways. I have always enjoyed the story of the two astronomers. One of them is crouched over, peering into the world's biggest telescope—an instrument the size of the Chrysler tower.

"It's going to rain," he says to his colleague.

"How can you tell?"

"My corns hurt."

The fear that scientific progress will bring about the slavery of man to machine has become more and more prevalent in this century. Some humorists have depicted man and machine as devoted enemies. In one of his standup routines, the contemporary comic Woody Allen, says, for example:

I have never had good relations with mechanical objects. . . . I have a clock that runs counterclockwise, and my toaster shakes my toast from side to side, and burns it, and I hate my shower. My shower hated me first, but then it got to be a thing of counter-hostility. If I'm taking a shower and someone in America uses their water, that's it for me! I leap from the tub with a red streak down my back. I paid $150 for a tape recorder, and as I talk into it, it goes "I know, I know!"

I have a Polaroid camera; it started putting out pictures in two minutes. I didn't want to say anything. Then it started putting out pictures in five minutes. Finally, I got a little note that said "Come in tomorrow for them!" So be nice to your camera.

The scientific revolution has led some spokesmen for our culture to declare that there has also been a revolution in morals, especially a sexual one. Great emphasis is now placed on sex appeal, but too many of us have sadly discovered that we don't live up to the high standards of beauty, virility, or charm promoted by the fashionable magazines. The discovery has led some humorists to find funny aspects of their inadequacy. The anti-hero, the loser, is learning how to fight back. Out of his determination has come a new kind of literature, the literature of the little man who conquers the massed legions of fashion, conformity, and pomposity—who beats the machine. It appears, in other words, as if we may be adjusting to this brave new world, just as we did a century ago to the frontier world. Just as Mark Twain was able to "put on" the establishment of his day, contemporary humorists are learning how to cope with the system on equal terms. Stephen Potter, in his books on one-up-manship, and Shepherd Mead, in his books on succeeding without even trying, are indicative of the needs of little men to even up the chances of success against the ponderous forces of science and society. Mead, for example, teaches boys how to succeed with women by practicing on their mothers:

> By following these simple rules you can make your mother useful and happy. She will thank you for it.
>
> You will not only be saving your strength and soothing your nerves, *you will be learning,* and what you learn in helping your mother will be valuable in dealing with other women.

However, remember this major difference between mothers and other females: Your mother is the only female who will want, from the start, to do something *for you.* Other women will always begin by wanting you to do something *for them.*

This is why it is so necessary to *bring out the mother* in all women as soon as possible. It is far easier to do than it sounds. . . .

HOW TO HANDLE TEACHERS

Luckily for you, most elementary school teachers are women. You can handle them just as easily as you do other women, and with the same methods.

Avoid the old cliches. For example, taking an apple to the teacher is bad. On the contrary:

"May I borrow your apple, Miss Brown?"

"Oh, Davie, are you so hungry?"

"Oh, no! We have plenty at home. Just felt a little weak."

(*Always be brave.*)

"You certainly *may* have my apple, Davie!"

Your object is *not* the apple. You may not even *like* apples. You are trying to win her friendship. She will soon forget the lad who *brought* the apple, but she will long remember the one who borrows it.

Our concern for improving our technology has resulted in our neglect of social conditions. The slum dweller cannot appreciate the launching of space satellites when he is out of work, the rent is due, and his scanty apartment is overrun with rats. The social discontent growing out of the Civil Rights movement has produced a humor, all too frequently bitter, that reminds us of the vast differences between the haves and the have nots. In fact, it might be said that the poor, the underprivileged, the member of a racial minority discriminated against, is in a way the frontiersman of modern times. In the humor of the underdog against the Establishment, of the poor against the rich, the Negro against the white man, can be seen elements of the rustic versus the over-civilized man—that oldest of American quarrels. Negro comedian Godfrey Cambridge, for example, suggests in "How To Hail a Cab in New York" ways in which a Negro can get a taxi:

> *Try and Look Innocent Method:* I stand there with a big broad smile on my face. I remove my sunglasses so no one thinks I'm a drug addict. I try to show them I'm a white Negro, carrying my attache case. I hail them with my attache case. They think I'm an executive. . . .
>
> *The Screaming-Friendly Approach:* I scream, "GOING DOWNTOWN, DOWNTOWN, DOWN. TOWN. I'M NOT GOING TO HARLEM!" . . .
>
> *The Money in the Hand Routine:* I have a $20.00 bill.

Godfrey Cambridge is in a way a frontiersman of modern times.

> Ha, torero! At the same time I wave a dollar bill in the other hand to show that I have change.
>
> *Rent-a-White Service:* If all these methods fail, you rent a white person for $2.00 an hour and all he has to do is hail cabs for you.

Another Negro comic, Dick Gregory, opens a routine this way:

> Isn't this the most fascinating country in the world? Where else would I have to ride on the back of the bus, have a choice of going to the worst schools, eating in the worst restaurants, living in the worst neighborhoods—and average $5000 a week just talking about it?

This turmoil in our social consciousness has signaled a revival in political humor, a brand that has not played a prominent part in our literature for some thirty years. As we have seen, disillusionment with the government was so strong in the 1930's that writers turned to smaller, more digestible aspects of their culture to pick on. Wartime conditions in the 1940's imposed informal censorship on writers who might otherwise poke fun at their government. And the so-called witch-hunt for communists instigated by Senator Joseph McCarthy in the 1950's intimidated political humorists. But the 1960's have seen the revival of political satire, perpetrated by such masters as Art Buchwald, Harry Golden, and Russell Baker.

One commentator, Merriman Smith, describes what he calls The Wonderful Washington Point System:

> Essentially, the point system is a conversational method of determining Washington status. Points are not necessarily cumulative. Perhaps the system is better described as a method of measurement or immediate appraisal. Something like a reviewer giving a movie two, three or four stars.

More than establishing rank or status, the point system is a way of expressing one's attitude toward a specific behaviorism or performance. Also, it may cover one's automobile, home, family or personal activities. . . .

Having the Schlesingers at a small dinner dance is good, provided there is an upstairs sitting room where brains of government may adjourn periodically to take telephone calls and talk about Adenauer or Vietnam. Since the Schlesingers do get around, however, this would not rate more than a point. If the Bundys were there, too, you might force it to two points, but not a whit more. . . .

Art Buchwald is probably the best-known of the political humorists, and the following passage from *I Chose Capitol Punishment* displays his delightful view of the international scene:

Every time things get quiet, or comparatively quiet, between East and West, the rumors start flying that Khrushchev is on his way out and that there is a new struggle in the Kremlin for power. In our own country when things quiet down, the rumors have it that President Kennedy will have no chance of getting his program through, and he is certain of being cut down on all his requests.

The sad fact, whether they like it or not, is that Khrushchev needs Kennedy and Kennedy needs Khrushchev, and I wouldn't be surprised if the "hot line" between Moscow and Washington serves a purpose other than to prevent accidental war.

I can imagine a conversation taking place between the two heads of state that might go something like this.

"Mr. Khrushchev, I'm sorry to bother you, but I was wondering when you were planning to send another man in orbit. I'm having a helluva time getting space funds. Is there any chance of getting a Russian up in space in the next two months?"

"We've been trying, but we've had some setbacks. You haven't been helping me much, you know, by postponing Cooper's flight. I'm having difficulty on funds also."

"I'm sorry about Cooper, Mr. Khrushchev, but we've had trouble with our booster. If you could send two or three men up right now, I'll do something spectacular for you when your next budget comes up."

Arthur C. Clarke, the science fiction writer, has written that the age of space exploration may bring about the greatest outburst of human creative energy since the Renaissance. It will be remembered that the Renaissance corresponded to, and was largely a product of, the great era of earth exploration. The old frontiers fell away then, leaving a huge void which men filled with their imaginations. So may modern frontiers fall away again as we strike out for the moon and beyond, plunge into the seas, or probe the stuff and the forces of nature. President John F. Kennedy, taking office in 1961, saw our task as the creation and conquest of New Frontiers. He realized that America's momentum depended on a process that promises breakthroughs in culture, art, and literature.

If the past experiences of this nation are any guide, the humor of the future will arise out of the disappointing contrasts we discover between the glories we expect from the New Frontiers, and the reality we encounter. We may strike farther and farther into the universe, perhaps colonizing the planets of our own and other stars; but as long as we are human beings there will always be surprising gaps between our hopes and their fulfillment. And as long as those gaps exist, they will have their Genial Idiots to make fun of them.

Bibliography

Note: The author read a large number of original sources in preparing this book, from which he selected the passages included. There is no better way for readers to follow up in areas in which they are interested than to read those original works, and read them in their original lengths. In the interests of keeping a reading list manageable, however, those works have been omitted in this bibliography. But the following books are suggested as good supplements for those wishing background:

Adler, Bill, ed. *Presidential Wit.* New York: Trident Press, 1966.

Aswell, James R., ed. *Native American Humor.* New York: Harper, 1947.

Austin, James C. *Artemus Ward.* New York: Twayne, 1964.

——— *Petroleum V. Nasby.* New York: Twayne, 1965.

Burnett, Whit, ed. *This Is My Best Humor.* New York: Dial Press, 1955.

Carlisle, Henry C., ed. *American Satire in Prose and Verse.* New York: Random House, 1962.

Cerf, Bennett, ed. *Encyclopaedia of Modern Humor.* Garden City, N.Y.: Doubleday, 1954.

Dudden, Arthur P., ed. *The Assault of Laughter.* New York: Yoseloff, 1962.

Fadiman, Clifton. *Enter, Conversing.* New York: World, 1962.

Falk, R. P., ed. *American Literature in Parody.* New York: Twayne, 1955.

Herzberg, Max J., ed. *Humor of America.* New York: Appleton-Century, 1945.

Hughes, Langston, ed. *The Book of Negro Humor.* New York: Dodd, Mead, 1967.

Love, Paula McSpadden: *The Will Rogers Book.* New York: Bobbs-Merrill, 1961.

Pattee, Fred Lewis, ed. *Century Readings in American Literature.* New York: Appleton-Century, 1912, 1932.

Playboy Magazine, editors of, ed. *Playboy Book of Humor & Satire.* Chicago: Playboy Press, 1967.

Rourke, Constance. *American Humor.* New York: Harcourt, Brace, 1931.

Simpson, Claude M., ed. *The Local Colorists.* New York: Harper, 1960.

Tidwell, James N., ed. *A Treasury of American Folk Humor.* New York: Crown, 1950.

Van Doren, Carl: *Benjamin Franklin.* New York: Viking Press, 1938.

Wagenknecht, Edward. *Washington Irving.* New York: Oxford University Press, 1962.

Weber, Brom, ed. *An Anthology of American Humor.* New York: Crowell, 1962.

Index

Index

INDEX